COOKIE COOKBOOK FOR BEC

© Copyright 2024 - All rights reserved.

The contents of this book may not be reproduced, duplicated, or transmitted without the direct written permission of the author or publisher.

Under no circumstances will the publisher or author be held liable for any damages, recovery, or financial loss due to the information contained in this book. Neither directly nor indirectly.

Legal Notice:

This book is protected by copyright. This book is for personal use only. You may not modify, distribute, sell, use, quote, or paraphrase any part or content of this book without the permission of the author or publisher.

Disclaimer Notice:

Please note that the information contained in this document is for educational and entertainment purposes only. Every effort has been made to present accurate, current, reliable, and complete information. No warranties of any kind are stated or implied. The reader acknowledges that the author is not offering legal, financial, medical, or professional advice. The contents of this book have been taken from various sources. Please consult a licensed professional before attempting any of the techniques described in this book.

By reading this document, the reader agrees that under no circumstances will the author be liable for any direct or indirect loss arising from the use of the information contained in this document, including but not limited to - errors, omissions, or inaccuracies.

TABLE OF CONTENTS

Chapter 1: Welcome To The World Of Cookies 3

Chapter 2: Essential Baking Tools And Ingredients 7

Chapter 3: Basic Baking Techniques 16

Chapter 4: Classic Cookie Types 24

Chapter 5: Cookie Troubleshooting 36

Chapter 6: Classic Cookie Creations 44

    1. Peanut Butter Cookies 44
    2. Sugar Cookies 45
    3. Snickerdoodles 47
    4. Chocolate Crinkle Cookies 48
    5. Gingerbread Crunch Cookies 49
    6. Classic Shortbread Cookies 51
    7. Classic Snickerdoodles 52
    8. Classic Thumbprint Cookies 53
    9. Classic Anzac Biscuits (Cookies) 54
    10. Classic Peanut Butter Blossom Cookies 55
    11. Classic Almond Biscotti 57
    12. Classic Coconut Macaroons 58
    13. Classic Linzer Cookies 59
    14. Classic Biscuit (Cookie) Sandwiches 60
    15. Classic Oatmeal Bars 61

Chapter 7: Flavorful Variations 63

    16. Apricot Thumbprint Cookies 63
    17. Gingersnap Cookies 64
    18. Coconut Macaroons 65
    19. Pecan Praline Cookies 66
    20. Anise Pizzelles 67

21.	Sugar Cookies	69
22.	Gingerbread Cookies	70
23.	Crispy Chocolate Chip Cookies	71
24.	Snickerdoodle Cookies	72
25.	Peanut Butter Blossoms	73
26.	Oatmeal Raisin Cookies	75
27.	Peppermint Chocolate Cookies	76
28.	Almond Snowball Cookies	77
29.	Pecan Sandies	78
30.	Lemon Shortbread Cookies	79
31.	Snowball Cookies	81
32.	Cherry Almond Cookies	82
33.	Chocolate Mint Cookies	83
34.	Cinnamon Sugar Cookies	84
35.	Cranberry Pistachio Biscotti	85

Chapter 8: Specialty Cookies **87**

36.	Raspberry Linzer Cookies	87
37.	Pistachio Cranberry Slice-And-Bake Cookies	88
38.	Lemon Meltaways	90
39.	Cherry Almond Biscotti	91
40.	Pomegranate White Chocolate Cookies	92
41.	Mocha Swirl Cookies	93
42.	Cinnamon Roll Cookies	95
43.	Tiramisu Cookies	96
44.	Chocolate Hazelnut Thumbprint Cookies	97
45.	Orange Cardamom Sable Cookies	98
46.	Caramel Apple Thumbprint Cookies	100
47.	Peppermint Bark Cookies	101
48.	Eggnog Snickerdoodles	102

49.	Chocolate-Dipped Almond Biscotti	103
50.	Maple Pecan Pie Cookies	105
51.	Cranberry Pistachio White Chocolate Chip Cookies	106
52.	Chocolate Peppermint Sandwich Cookies	107
53.	Orange Cranberry Shortbread Cookies	109
54.	Mint Chocolate Crinkle Cookies	110
55.	Chocolate Caramel Thumbprint Cookies	111

Chapter 9: Healthy And Gluten-Free Options 113

56.	Almond Flour Chocolate Chip Cookies	113
57.	Coconut Macaroons	114
58.	Gluten-Free Oatmeal Cookies	115
59.	Quinoa Chocolate Cookies	117
60.	Gluten-Free Peanut Butter Cookies	118
61.	Gluten-Free Banana Cookies	118
62.	Gluten-Free Coconut Flour Sugar Cookies	120
63.	Gluten-Free Zucchini Chocolate Chip Cookies	121
64.	Gluten-Free Chickpea Chocolate Cookies	122
65.	Gluten-Free Banana Oatmeal Breakfast Cookies	123
66.	Sparkling Cookies	125
67.	Vanilla Cookies	126
68.	Classic Snowman Cookies	127
69.	Blub Cookies	128
70.	Royal Cookies	129

Conclusion 131

CHAPTER 1

WELCOME TO THE WORLD OF COOKIES

In the warm embrace of your kitchen, a world of sweet delights awaits you. Baking cookies is not merely a culinary endeavor; it's a sensory journey. The scent of butter and vanilla dancing in the air, the rhythmic whir of the mixer, and the transformation of humble ingredients into delectable morsels of comfort – this is the joy of baking.

Baking cookies transcends the boundaries of age, culture, and experience. It's a universal language of love, expressed through the act of creation. Every step, from measuring out ingredients to watching the dough transform into delicate rounds of potential, is a moment to savor.

The Joy of Baking is not just about the final product, but the entire process. It's about sifting flour with anticipation, gently folding in chocolate chips, and the rewarding feeling of pulling a batch of golden-brown cookies from the oven. The warmth, the aroma, and the taste of freshly baked cookies connect us to cherished memories and create new ones.

This chapter is your gateway to the enchanting world of cookies. Here, you'll learn not just the recipes but the art and science behind baking. As you embark on this journey, remember that every cookie you bake carries a piece of your heart, making it an edible gift, a small token of love to be shared with family, friends, or simply enjoyed in solitude.

The Joy of Baking is about much more than satisfying your sweet tooth; it's about discovering the joy in the process, the comfort in tradition, and the delight in sharing. So, let's roll up our sleeves, Heat in advance the oven, and embark on this delectable adventure together. Welcome to the world of cookies, where joy is the main ingredient.

- **Why Cookies?**

Cookies have a unique place in the world of baking. They are simple yet versatile, familiar yet endlessly customizable, and they hold a special spot in our hearts. But why cookies, you might wonder? What is it about these small, round treats that makes them so beloved?

Cookies are a universal delight. They have the power to bring a smile to faces young and old, bridging generational gaps and cultural differences. Whether it's the nostalgia of grandma's secret recipe or the comforting aroma that fills the kitchen, cookies have an uncanny ability to create a sense of home and warmth.

Cookies are quick to make and quick to enjoy. In a world that often moves too fast, cookies provide a delicious shortcut to satisfaction. Unlike complex cakes or multi-layered pastries, cookies offer a speedy route to sweet gratification. With a few basic ingredients and minimal prep time, you can transform your kitchen into a fragrant bakery.

Cookies are endlessly customizable. From classic chocolate chip to innovative flavor combinations, cookies can be adapted to suit any taste or occasion. Want a dash of cinnamon and a sprinkle of sea salt? How about adding nuts, dried fruit, or even a hint of espresso? Cookies welcome your creativity with open arms.

Cookies are perfect for sharing. They are the ultimate gesture of generosity and care. A plate of freshly baked cookies can turn an ordinary day into a memorable one, making them perfect for celebrations, gatherings, or as a thoughtful gift to brighten someone's day.

Cookies are a canvas for your baking journey. As a beginner, cookies provide a gentle introduction to the world of baking. They allow you to practice key techniques, experiment with ingredients, and gain confidence in your culinary skills.

So, why cookies? Because they are a joyful, versatile, and universally loved treat that connects us to our past and paves the way for new culinary adventures. In the pages that follow, you'll discover not only the 'how' but also the 'why' of baking cookies. Welcome to a world where cookies aren't just a dessert; they're a delightful expression of creativity and connection.

- **A Baker's Journey**

Every baker, no matter their level of experience, embarks on a unique journey. The act of baking is not merely about creating delicious treats; it's a voyage of self-discovery, growth, and endless learning. This chapter is not a set of instructions but a glimpse into the profound and personal journey of a baker.

The journey begins with a spark of curiosity or a cherished family tradition. Perhaps it's the memory of your grandmother's warm, freshly baked cookies, or maybe it's the desire to create something beautiful and delicious with your own hands. This initial inspiration is the foundation upon which your baking adventure is built.

As you take your first steps in the world of baking, you'll encounter ingredients that were once strangers – flour, sugar, eggs, and butter. With each measurement, each whisk of the bowl, you'll become more acquainted with their nuances, textures, and behaviors. You'll start to understand that the science of baking is a harmonious blend of precision and creativity.

Your journey may include missteps and flops, cookies that are too crispy or too chewy, and moments when the dough doesn't quite behave as expected. But don't be discouraged; these are not failures but lessons. Each experience, whether sweet or slightly bitter, adds to your baking repertoire.

Over time, your kitchen will become a laboratory, and the recipes mere suggestions. You'll experiment with flavors, tweak techniques, and craft your unique signature cookies. Baking will become an art form, a form of self-expression that carries your emotions, creativity, and care.

As you hone your skills, the joy of baking will extend beyond your kitchen. You'll find it in the delighted smiles of those you share your cookies with, in the warm feeling of nostalgia they evoke, and in the connections you forge with fellow bakers, both novice and experienced.

Your journey as a baker is ongoing, a path of constant discovery and growth. It's a pursuit of perfection, though you know it's the imperfections that make each cookie uniquely yours. Through the highs and lows, you'll come to understand that baking isn't just about creating delectable treats; it's about the personal transformation that occurs with each batch.

As you delve into the pages of this book, remember that you are not just following recipes; you're continuing your journey as a baker, each chapter a new mile marker on your path of exploration and delight. Welcome to your unique, ever-evolving baker's journey.

CHAPTER 2
ESSENTIAL BAKING TOOLS AND INGREDIENTS

- **Must-Have Baking Tools**

In the enchanting world of baking, your kitchen becomes your sanctuary, and the tools you choose to use are your trusted companions on a journey of creativity and deliciousness. Every baker, from novice to expert, knows that the right tools are essential to achieving baking perfection. In this chapter, we'll delve into the must-have baking tools that will transform your kitchen into a cookie-baking haven.

1. **Measuring Cupful and Spoons:** Precision is the cornerstone of baking, and it all starts with accurate measurements. A reliable set of measuring cupful and spoons will ensure that you're adding just the right amount of flour, sugar, and other ingredients to your cookie dough.

2. **Mixing Bowls:** Baking is an art of precision and combining various ingredients harmoniously. A set of different-sized mixing bowls is invaluable. Whether you're sifting flour, whisking eggs, or mixing wet and dry ingredients, these bowls provide the canvas for your culinary creations. Durable stainless steel or transparent glass bowls are excellent choices.

3. **Whisk:** A whisk is a versatile tool that serves multiple purposes in baking. It helps you blend dry ingredients, beat eggs, and incorporate air into your batter, resulting in light and fluffy cookies.

4. **Stand Mixer or Hand Mixer:** While many recipes can be mixed by hand, an electric mixer can save you time and effort, especially when working with larger batches or recipes that require extended mixing. A stand mixer with various attachments is a baker's dream for tackling tasks like creaming butter and sugar.

5. **Spatula:** A good spatula is a must-have for every baker. It's perfect for folding delicate ingredients, scraping every bit of dough from the bowl, and transferring batter into the baking dish. Silicone spatulas are heat-resistant, making them ideal for use with hot ingredients, and they're a breeze to clean.

6. **Baking Sheets:** Baking sheets are essential for uniformly baking your cookies. Opt for sturdy, rimmed baking sheets that can withstand the heat of your oven. To prevent cookies from baring and simplify cleanup, consider using parchment paper or silicone baking mats.

7. **Cooling Rack:** A cooling rack is the unsung hero of cookie baking. Placing your freshly baked cookies on a rack ensures they cool evenly, preventing them from becoming soggy on the bottom.

8. **Cookie Scoops:** These handy tools come in various sizes and ensure that your cookies are uniform in size, which is not only visually appealing but also crucial for even baking. They also help you portion out the dough with minimal mess.

9. **Rolling Pin:** For rolled cookies and dough, a rolling pin is indispensable. It allows you to achieve the desired thickness, ensuring your cookies bake evenly.

10. **Cookie Cutters:** These come in various shapes and sizes, allowing you to create decorative and personalized cookies. Cookie cutters are a fantastic way to express your creativity and make your cookies stand out.

11. **Pastry Brush:** A pastry brush is a valuable tool for adding that finishing touch to your cookies. Whether you're applying an egg wash, brushing cookies with melted butter, or adding glazes, a pastry brush ensures precise and even application.

12. **Oven Thermometer:** Baking is all about precision, and maintaining the correct temperature is crucial for successful cookie baking. An oven thermometer will ensure your oven is at the exact temperature specified in your recipes, preventing over- or under-baking.

13. **Timer:** The ability to keep track of baking times is a baker's best friend. A reliable kitchen timer helps you ensure that your cookies are baked to perfection and prevents them from burning.

14. **Silicone Baking Mat:** These reusable mats are an eco-friendly alternative to parchment paper. Not only do they promote sustainability, but they also help cookies bake evenly and prevent baring.

15. **Cooling Rack:** Elevating your cookies on a cooling rack allows for better airflow, ensuring they cool evenly and maintain their desired texture, whether that's crispy, chewy, or somewhere in between.

16. **Pastry Bags and Tips:** If you plan on taking your cookie baking to the next level by decorating your cookies with icing, a set of pastry bags and tips is indispensable. These tools allow you to create intricate designs, patterns, and decorations that turn your cookies into edible works of art.

Arming yourself with these must-have baking tools is not just about convenience; it's about ensuring your success in the kitchen. These tools will make your cookie-baking experience more efficient, enjoyable, and, most importantly, will help you achieve delicious, consistent results. As you embark on your journey to explore the world of cookies, consider these essential tools your reliable companions, supporting you in creating delectable, memorable treats with every batch.

- **Key Baking Ingredients**

In the realm of baking, ingredients are like characters in a story. Each has a role to play, a unique personality, and when combined artfully, they create the perfect narrative – or in this case, a delectable batch of cookies. Let's explore these key ingredients, uncover their nuances, and understand the magic they bring to the world of baking.

1. **Flour:** Flour is the backbone of most cookie recipes, providing structure and texture. It comes in various types, such as all-purpose, bread, pastry, and cake flour. The protein content in flour influences the texture of your cookies. Higher protein flours like bread flour result in chewier cookies, while lower protein flours like cake flour create a more delicate, tender crumb.

2. **Sugar:** Sugar isn't just about sweetness; it contributes to the texture, moisture retention, and browning of your cookies. Granulated sugar is the standard, but brown sugar adds a deeper, caramel-like flavor, and confectioners' sugar (powdered sugar) is

used for delicate, melt-in-the-mouth textures. Experimenting with specialty sugars like demerara or turbinado can add a layer of complexity to your cookies.

3. **Butter:** Butter is the superstar of many cookie recipes, infusing them with flavor, moisture, and a tender crumb. Unsalted butter is often the preferred choice in baking, as it allows for better control of the salt content in your cookies. If you use salted butter, adjustments may be needed in your recipe.

4. **Eggs:** Eggs are the multi-talented ingredients in your baking toolkit. They act as both binders and leavening agents, providing structure and lift to your cookies. Eggs also contribute moisture and richness, enhancing both the texture and flavor of your creations. Fresh, large eggs are the standard for most cookie recipes.

5. **Leavening Agents:** Baking powder and baking soda are common leavening agents that make your cookies rise. Baking powder contains both an acid and a base and is often used in recipes that don't already contain an acid. Baking soda, on the other hand, requires an acid, such as brown sugar or buttermilk, to activate its leavening properties.

6. **Salt:** Salt is the unsung hero in baking. While it may seem counterintuitive to add salt to sweet recipes, it enhances the overall flavor by balancing the sweetness and other tastes. It's a crucial element that should not be omitted, even in sweet cookie recipes.

7. **Vanilla Extract:** Vanilla extract is like the background music in a film, creating depth and ambiance. It adds a rich, warm, and slightly sweet flavor to your cookies. Pure vanilla extract is the preferred choice for its authentic and robust flavor.

8. **Chocolate Chips or Chunks:** Chocolate chips or chunks are the pièce de résistance for many cookie recipes. Whether you prefer dark, semi-sweet, or milk

chocolate, these morsels create gooey, melty pockets of chocolatey goodness, elevating your cookies to another level of indulgence.

9. **Nuts:** Chopped nuts, such as walnuts, pecans, or almonds, can add a delightful crunch and nutty flavor to your cookies. While these are often optional, they can significantly enhance the texture and taste of your creations.

10. **Dried Fruits:** Raisins, cranberries, apricots, or other dried fruits introduce a burst of sweetness and chewiness to your cookies. They're a versatile addition, allowing you to experiment with different flavor profiles.

11. **Spices:** Spices like cinnamon, nutmeg, and cloves can infuse your cookies with warmth and complexity. They create a comforting and aromatic quality that makes your cookies truly unforgettable.

12. **Decorative Elements:** For special occasions or just to add a touch of whimsy, consider decorative elements like sprinkles, colored sugars, or edible decorations. They not only make your cookies visually appealing but also set the tone for different occasions or themes.

13. **Flavorings:** Beyond vanilla extract, you might explore other flavorings like almond extract, lemon zest, or orange extract. These additions introduce unique flavor profiles to your cookies, allowing you to experiment and create cookies with distinct personalities.

Each of these key ingredients is a crucial component of your baking adventures. Understanding their roles, characteristics, and interactions will empower you to experiment, innovate, and create your signature cookies. The world of cookies is a canvas, and these ingredients are the paints that allow you to craft your own culinary masterpieces. In the pages that follow, you'll see how these elements come together in various recipes, weaving a tapestry of flavors, textures, and delights.

- **Baking Substitutions**

In the enchanting world of baking, being able to adapt and overcome is a valuable skill. Sometimes, in the midst of your culinary masterpiece, you may realize that you're missing a crucial ingredient. It's in these moments that knowledge of baking substitutions becomes your secret weapon. Whether it's due to dietary restrictions, ingredient shortages, or simply a desire to experiment, understanding how to swap one ingredient for another can be a game-changer in your baking endeavors.

1. **Flour Substitutions:**

- All-Purpose Flour: The most versatile of flours, all-purpose flour, can often be swapped with other types to achieve unique textures and flavors. Whole wheat flour adds a nutty, hearty element, while cake flour produces a lighter, more delicate crumb.

- Gluten-Free Flour: For those with gluten sensitivities, an array of gluten-free flour blends is available, allowing you to enjoy your favorite cookies without the gluten.

2. **Sugar Substitutions:**

- Granulated Sugar: In most recipes, granulated sugar can be replaced with brown sugar to impart a deeper, more caramel-like flavor. If you're looking for a natural sweetener, honey, maple syrup, or agave nectar can be used, though it's important to adjust the liquid and sugar ratios in your recipe accordingly.

- Confectioners' Sugar: When you find yourself without confectioners' sugar, don't fret. You can make your own by blending granulated sugar with a touch of cornstarch in a food processor until it reaches a finely powdered consistency.

3. **Butter Substitutions:**

- Unsalted Butter: If you're out of unsalted butter, salted butter can often be used as a substitute, with the understanding that you may need to adjust the recipe's salt content accordingly. You can also explore alternatives such as vegetable oil, coconut oil, or even applesauce for lower-fat options.

4. **Egg Substitutions:**

- Eggs: In recipes where eggs serve as binders, you can get creative with substitutes. Mashed bananas or applesauce work well. For leavening, yogurt, buttermilk, or a mixture of water, oil, and baking powder can fill the void.

- Vegan Options: For vegan baking, you have a plethora of options, including commercial egg replacers or the classic flaxseed and water mixture.

5. **Leavening Agent Substitutions:**

- Baking Powder: If you've run out of baking powder, you can create a makeshift version by combining cream of tartar and baking soda. In dire straits, self-rising flour can also be used as a substitute (bearing in mind that it contains salt, so adjust the recipe's salt content).

- Baking Soda: When out of baking soda, you can usually replace it with baking powder, although you'll need to use three times the amount specified for baking soda in the recipe.

6.

7. **Salt Substitutions:**

• Sometimes, you may need to reduce salt due to dietary preferences or restrictions. In such cases, explore alternative flavor enhancers. Herbs, spices, and umami-rich ingredients like soy sauce, miso, or Parmesan cheese can add depth and complexity to your cookies without increasing the saltiness.

8. **Milk Substitutions:**

• Dairy Milk: In recipes that call for dairy milk, you can often use almond milk, soy milk, coconut milk, or oat milk as suitable alternatives. These substitutions can accommodate dietary preferences or restrictions.

• Buttermilk: When you don't have buttermilk on hand, a simple substitute is to mix regular milk with vinegar or lemon juice. The acid in these ingredients mimics the tangy flavor of buttermilk.

9. **Vanilla Extract Substitutions:**

• Vanilla extract, a staple in many recipes, can be replaced with vanilla bean paste, vanilla powder, or even almond extract for a different flavor profile. Each of these alternatives imparts its unique aroma and taste, allowing you to customize your cookies to your liking.

10. **Chocolate Chip Substitutions:**

• While chocolate chips are the beloved inclusion in many cookies, you can experiment with various types and combinations to suit your taste. Dark, semi-sweet, or milk chocolate chips and even white chocolate can all create distinct flavors and textures in your cookies.

11. **Nuts and Dried Fruit Substitutions:**

- Nuts and dried fruit can add texture and flavor to your cookies, but these elements are often optional. You can replace one type of nut with another or even experiment with seeds. When it comes to dried fruits, personal preference and availability can guide your choices.

11. **Spice Substitutions:**

- Spices are another opportunity to customize your cookies. You can swap one spice for another or adjust the quantities to suit your palate and create your unique flavor profile.

Understanding baking substitutions opens a world of possibilities in your cookie-baking journey. It allows you to adapt recipes to suit your preferences, accommodate dietary needs, or make the most of the ingredients you have on hand. Remember that while substitutions can work in many cases, they may slightly alter the taste, texture, or appearance of your cookies. It's always a good idea to make a small test batch to evaluate the results before committing to a full batch. With practice, you'll become a master of adaptation, turning each batch of cookies into a personalized creation that suits your tastes and dietary requirements. Substitutions are the gateway to a world of creative baking, allowing you to craft cookies that are uniquely your own.

CHAPTER 3
BASIC BAKING TECHNIQUES

- **Measuring Like a Pro**

In the world of baking, precision is paramount. Accurate measurements are the foundation of successful cookies. Whether you're a novice or an experienced baker, mastering the art of measuring like a pro is essential. This chapter is your guide to ensuring that every ingredient is weighed or spooned out with precision, resulting in cookies that are consistent, delicious, and a testament to your baking prowess.

1. **Using the Right Tools:**

- Invest in high-quality measuring cupful and spoons made of metal or sturdy plastic. Make sure they have clear, easy-to-read markings. A kitchen scale is also an invaluable tool for precise measurements, especially for ingredients like flour and sugar.

2. **Flour:**

- Fluff the flour in its container before scooping it into your measuring cup. Gently spoon the flour into the cupful without tapping it or shaking it. Level the top with a flat-edged utensil, like the back of a knife, to ensure you're not inadvertently packing in more flour.

3. **Brown Sugar:**

- When measuring brown sugar, spoon it into the measuring cup, allowing it to lightly pack. Level it off with a straight-edged utensil. For an extra pro tip, if your brown sugar is clumpy, you can break up the lumps by pressing them through a sieve.

4. **Granulated Sugar:**

- Simply spoon granulated sugar into the measuring cupful and level it off. There's no need to pack it as you would with brown sugar.

5. **Butter:**

- Measure butter by filling a liquid measuring cupful with the required amount of water. Add small pieces of butter until the water level reaches the desired measurement. This method ensures that the butter is measured by displacement, accounting for air pockets.

6. **Liquids:**

- Use a liquid measuring cupful to measure liquids like milk, oil, or vanilla extract. Read the measurement at eye level to ensure accuracy. For bary liquids like honey, you can lightly grease the measuring cupful or spoon with cooking spray to prevent baring.

7. **Eggs:**

- Crack eggs into a separate container before adding them to your mixing bowl. This prevents shell fragments from finding their way into your dough and allows you to remove any bad eggs without ruining the entire batch.

8. **Leavening Agents:**

- For baking powder and baking soda, use dry measuring cups, and level them off with a straight-edged utensil. Ensure they are fresh and not expired, as they lose their leavening power over time.

9. **Spices:**

- Use dry measuring spoons for spices, leveling them off with a knife. Remember that spices lose flavor over time, so ensure they are fresh for the best results.

10. **Chocolate Chips and Mix-Ins:**

- Measure mix-ins, like chocolate chips or nuts, by lightly spooning them into the measuring cupful and leveling them off. Don't shake the cupful to pack them in, as this can lead to inaccurate measurements.

11. **Sifting:**

- Sifting dry ingredients, such as flour, cocoa, or powdered sugar, is an additional step that ensures uniform distribution and aerates the ingredients. Sift into a dry measuring cupful or a bowl, and then level it off.

12. **Measuring Odd Quantities:**

- For smaller quantities of ingredients, like a fraction of a teaspoon, invest in a set of measuring spoons that includes odd measurements. This will help you accurately measure minute amounts.

13. **Practice and Consistency:**

- Consistency is key. Always measure ingredients in the same way to ensure your results are reproducible. Practice your measuring techniques to become more confident and precise over time.

Mastering the art of measuring is an essential skill in your cookie-baking repertoire. Accurate measurements are the bedrock of consistent and delicious results. Whether you're following a classic recipe or experimenting with your own creations, measuring like a pro ensures that your cookies will turn out just as you envisioned, every time. So, arm yourself with the right tools, practice your techniques, and let precision be your guiding star as you embark on your baking journey.

- **Mixing, Stirring, and Folding**

In the magical realm of baking, the creation of perfect cookies isn't solely about the ingredients; it's also about how you handle them. The techniques you employ when mixing, stirring, and folding are like the artist's brush strokes, imparting a unique character and texture to your cookie creations. In this chapter, we delve deeper into the art and science of mixing, stirring, and folding, equipping you with the knowledge and skills needed to craft cookies that are not merely good but truly spectacular.

Mixing Methods:

1. **Creaming:** Creaming is a fundamental technique in cookie baking, especially for classics like chocolate chip cookies. It involves beating softened butter and sugar until the mixture becomes light, fluffy, and pale. This creamed mixture traps air,

creating tiny pockets that allow cookies to rise and become tender. For ideal creaming, the butter should be at room temperature.

2. **Melt and Mix:** Some cookies, like no-bake treats or certain bar cookies, follow the "melt and mix" method. This entails melting ingredients such as butter and chocolate together and then incorporating the dry ingredients. The result is often a rich, fudgy texture.

3. **One-Bowl Method:** For those who appreciate simplicity and efficiency, some cookie recipes are designed for the one-bowl method. In this approach, all ingredients are combined in a single bowl, which is ideal for quick, no-fuss cookies. It's a time-saving and straightforward way to make a delicious batch.

Stirring Techniques:

4. **Stirring:** Stirring is a method used to gently combine ingredients in your cookie dough. A wooden spoon or a rubber spatula is often the tool of choice. This technique is perfect for integrating mix-ins like chocolate chips, dried fruits, or nuts. It's crucial not to overmix, as this can lead to tough cookies.

5. **Folding:** Folding is a technique often employed when incorporating delicate ingredients like whipped egg whites or whipped cream into cookie batter. It's a gentle, careful process where you lift and fold the ingredients together until they are evenly blended. The goal is to avoid deflating the whipped elements, ensuring a light and airy texture in the finished product.

Mixing Tools:

6. **Wooden Spoon:** A wooden spoon is a versatile tool for stirring cookie dough. Its sturdy construction can handle thicker batters and provides excellent control.

7. **Rubber Spatula:** A rubber spatula is perfect for folding in ingredients and scraping every bit of dough from the bowl. Its flexibility is gentle on the dough, preventing overmixing.

8. **Stand Mixer or Hand Mixer:** For recipes that require creaming butter and sugar, an electric mixer is a time-saving ally. It ensures that the mixture is thoroughly creamed, aerating it to perfection.

9. **Whisk:** A whisk is a go-to tool for blending dry ingredients and ensuring they are uniformly mixed before incorporating them into the wet ingredients. It also comes in handy when breaking up clumps in ingredients like cocoa powder or brown sugar.

Mixing Techniques:

10. **Dry Ingredients First:** In most recipes, it's a recommended practice to combine dry ingredients in a separate bowl before adding them to the wet ingredients. This ensures an even distribution of leavening agents, preventing clumps and ensuring consistent results.

11. **Gradual Additions:** When incorporating dry ingredients into wet ingredients, do so gradually. Mix a little at a time, alternating with any liquid components. This approach helps in achieving a smooth, homogeneous dough while avoiding overmixing.

12. **Low Speed:** If you're using an electric mixer, especially for creaming butter and sugar, start at a low speed. This prevents the flour from flying out of the bowl and provides better control. Gradually increase the speed as the ingredients combine.

Overmixing and Undermixing:

13. **Overmixing:** Overmixing can lead to tough cookies due to the development of excess gluten. It's crucial to stop mixing as soon as the ingredients are combined, ensuring a tender and delicate texture.

14. **Undermixing:** On the other hand, undermixing can result in uneven cookies with pockets of flour. It's essential to ensure that all ingredients are fully combined to avoid a grainy or lumpy texture. Achieving the perfect balance is key.

Mix-Ins:

15. **Mix-Ins:** When adding ingredients such as chocolate chips, nuts, or dried fruits, gently fold them into the dough. This guarantees that they are evenly distributed without overmixing. Overmixing can cause the mix-ins to break apart or become unevenly distributed in the dough.

Chilling the Dough:

16. **Chilling the Dough:** Some cookie recipes benefit from chilling the dough before baking. This step solidifies the fat in the dough, preventing cookies from spreading too much during baking and resulting in thicker, chewier cookies. Chilling also allows the flavors to meld and intensify.

Mixing, stirring, and folding are the unsung heroes of cookie baking, akin to the precise brushwork of a master artist. The right techniques and tools ensure that your cookies turn out as envisioned – perfectly textured and flavorful. By understanding and mastering these methods, you can take your cookie creations to the next level, confidently experimenting with various recipes and techniques to achieve the desired results.

As you embark on your cookie-baking journey, remember that practice is your best teacher. The more you experiment and hone your skills, the more you'll appreciate the art of mixing, stirring, and folding. These techniques are the secret to crafting cookies that not only taste divine but also have that irresistible texture and character that makes them truly exceptional. Happy mixing and folding!

- **The Science of Baking**

Baking is a blend of art and science, where understanding the chemical reactions and physical transformations that occur during the baking process is the key to mastering the craft. In this chapter, we embark on a journey into the science of baking, unraveling the mysteries that occur within your cookie dough as it transforms from a simple mixture of ingredients into a delectable treat.

1. **Leavening Agents:** Leavening agents are the magical ingredients that make your cookies rise. Two common leavening agents are baking powder and baking soda. Baking powder contains both an acid and a base, while baking soda is a base that requires an acid to activate. When these substances react with moisture and heat, they release carbon dioxide gas, causing the dough to expand, resulting in light, airy cookies.

2. **Gluten Formation:** Gluten is a protein that forms when water is mixed with flour. Kneading or overmixing dough promotes gluten development, making it stretchy and elastic. In cookies, you want minimal gluten formation for a tender texture. That's why you're advised to mix cookie dough until just combined to avoid toughness.

3. **Fats:** Fats, like butter, play multiple roles in baking. They coat the flour particles, inhibiting gluten formation and resulting in tender cookies. Fats also trap air during the creaming process, aiding in the cookie's rise and contributing to its texture. Additionally, fats lend flavor and moisture to your cookies.

4. **Sugar:** Sugar isn't merely a sweetener; it's a master of texture, too. When sugar is mixed with butter, it creates small air pockets, making the cookies light and tender. Sugar also contributes to moisture retention and enhances browning during baking. The type and amount of sugar you use can dramatically affect your cookies' texture and appearance.

5. **Eggs:** Eggs are multifunctional in baking. They serve as binders, holding the ingredients together, and as leavening agents, contributing to a cookie's rise. Eggs also add moisture and richness to the dough, impacting its texture and flavor.

6. **Temperature:** Baking temperatures are critical. When the dough is placed in the oven, the heat causes the leavening agents to release gas, expanding the dough. The proteins, fats, and sugars set, creating structure and texture. The browning reactions, like the Maillard reaction, add color and depth to your cookies.

7. **Cookie Thickness:** The thickness of your cookies can be controlled by adjusting ingredients like flour, fats, and leavening agents. Reducing the flour and increasing fats and leavening agents results in a thinner, chewier cookie, while increasing the flour and reducing fats and leavening agents produces a thicker, cakier cookie.

8. **Mix-Ins:** The type and amount of mix-ins, such as chocolate chips, nuts, or dried fruits, can affect the texture, flavor, and appearance of your cookies. Experimenting with different mix-ins allows you to create unique cookie variations.

9. **Resting and Chilling:** Allowing the cookie dough to rest or chill in the refrigerator before baking can yield significant results. It allows the ingredients to meld, intensifying flavors, and it can also control the spreading of cookies during baking, giving you more control over their shape and texture.

10. **Time and Precision:** Baking is a precise science. Measuring your ingredients accurately, observing bake times, and controlling temperature are critical. Small deviations can significantly impact your cookies' outcome.

Understanding the science of baking empowers you to confidently adapt and experiment with cookie recipes, creating cookies that match your personal preferences. Whether you desire a chewy, thin, crispy, or cakey texture, or if you prefer a certain level of sweetness or browning, this knowledge equips you to become a cookie scientist in your own kitchen. As you continue your journey in the world of cookies, remember that science and art coalesce to produce cookies that are not only visually appealing but also irresistibly delicious. Happy baking!

CHAPTER 4
CLASSIC COOKIE TYPES

- **Chocolate Chip Cookies**

Chocolate chip cookies are the quintessential classic that warms hearts and delights taste buds. Their irresistible aroma wafting from the oven and the gooey, melty chocolate chips make them a favorite among cookie enthusiasts. In this chapter, we delve into the iconic chocolate chip cookie, exploring its history, ingredients, and the secrets to crafting the perfect batch.

1. **History of the Chocolate Chip Cookie:**

- The story of the chocolate chip cookie is a sweet and serendipitous one. Ruth Wakefield, the owner of the Toll House Inn, accidentally invented the chocolate chip cookie in the 1930s when she substituted chunks of a Nestlé semi-sweet chocolate bar into her butter cookie recipe. The result was a sensation, and the Toll House chocolate chip cookie was born.

2. **The Perfect Chocolate Chip Cookie:**

- Achieving the perfect chocolate chip cookie involves balancing various elements. From the right ratio of ingredients to the precise cooking time, it's a blend of science and art. Key factors include the type of chocolate, the texture (chewy or crispy), and the balance of sweetness.

3. **Ingredients for Classic Chocolate Chip Cookies:**

- **Butter:** Butter is the star ingredient, offering flavor, moisture, and a rich, creamy texture. Unsalted butter is often preferred to control the cookie's saltiness.

- **Sugars:** A combination of granulated sugar and brown sugar lends sweetness and texture. Brown sugar contributes to moisture and caramel notes, while granulated sugar offers a crisp edge.

- **Eggs:** Eggs serve as binders, providing structure and moisture.

- **Vanilla Extract:** A touch of vanilla extract enhances the flavor of the cookie.

- **Flour:** All-purpose flour is the base, but experimenting with different types can create varied textures.

- **Baking Soda and Baking Powder:** These leavening agents help the cookies rise, giving them a soft, tender interior.

- **Salt:** A pinch of salt balances the sweetness and enhances flavor.

- **Chocolate Chips:** Semi-sweet or dark chocolate chips are commonly used, but you can also explore milk chocolate, white chocolate, or even a blend for different flavor profiles.

4. **Texture Variations:**

- Chocolate chip cookies offer a spectrum of textures, from soft and chewy to crispy. Adjusting the ingredients, such as the sugar and fat ratios, and experimenting with baking times, can tailor the texture to your liking.

5. **Mixing Techniques:**

- Creaming the butter and sugar is a classic step in making chocolate chip cookies. This creates air pockets and contributes to the cookie's tenderness. The dry ingredients are typically mixed separately and then added to the wet mixture, ensuring even distribution.

6. **The Science of Melting Chocolate:**

- Achieving those gooey, melty chocolate pockets in your cookies is an art and a science. Understanding the melting points of different chocolate types and adjusting your recipe accordingly is key to perfecting the texture.

7. **Secret Tips for Chocolate Chip Cookies:**

- A few secrets, such as chilling the dough before baking or underbaking slightly, can elevate your chocolate chip cookies to the next level.

8. **Variations and Add-Ins:**

- Chocolate chip cookies offer endless opportunities for customization. You can add nuts, dried fruits, or spices to create your signature version of this classic.

9. **Classic vs. Modern Recipes:**

- While the classic Toll House chocolate chip cookie recipe is beloved, modern variations have emerged, often experimenting with ingredients like browned butter, sea salt, or different types of chocolate for a unique twist on tradition.

Chocolate chip cookies are more than just a sweet treat; they're a piece of nostalgia, a symbol of comfort, and a canvas for your creativity. In this chapter, we explore the classic chocolate chip cookie and all the nuances that can elevate it to perfection. As you embark on your cookie-baking journey, remember that there's no one-size-fits-all recipe. Your ideal chocolate chip cookie may be chewy, crispy, loaded with nuts, or swirled with different types of chocolate. It's all about crafting a cookie that suits your taste and brings joy to those who enjoy it. Happy baking!

- **Sugar Cookies**

Sugar cookies are the canvas of the cookie world, offering endless possibilities for artistic expression and sweet indulgence. In this chapter, we explore the world of sugar cookies, from their versatile base recipe to the art of decorating and making them your own.

1. **The Timeless Allure of Sugar Cookies:**

- Sugar cookies have been a beloved treat for generations. Their simple yet delightful flavor is a hallmark of the holidays and special occasions, making them a favorite canvas for cookie decorators and enthusiasts.

2. **Ingredients for Sugar Cookies:**

- Sugar cookies require just a handful of simple ingredients:
- **Butter:** Provides rich flavor and tenderness.

- **Sugar:** Sweetens the dough and contributes to the cookie's texture.
- **Egg:** Acts as a binder, adding moisture and structure.
- **Vanilla Extract:** Enhances the flavor.
- **Flour:** Forms the base of the dough.
- **Baking Powder:** Provides leavening for a tender texture.
- **Salt:** Balances sweetness and enhances flavor.

3. **The Science of Rolling and Cutting:**

- Sugar cookie dough is unique because it's firm enough to be rolled out and cut into various shapes. Understanding the dough's texture and temperature is essential for successful rolling and cutting.

4. **Flavor Variations:**

- Sugar cookies can be customized with various flavorings such as almond extract, lemon zest, or spices like cinnamon and nutmeg, providing endless options for personalization.

5. **Decorating Sugar Cookies:**

- Decorating sugar cookies is an art form. Whether it's a simple glaze, royal icing, or intricate piping, this chapter explores the techniques, tools, and tips for achieving professional-looking designs on your sugar cookies.

6. **Royal Icing:**

- Royal icing is the go-to choice for many sugar cookie decorators. It dries hard, creating a smooth canvas for intricate designs and patterns.

7. **Texture Variations:**

• Adjusting the ingredients, such as sugar and butter ratios, can create sugar cookies with varying textures, from soft and tender to crisper and more delicate.

8. **Flavored Icing and Fillings:**

• Sugar cookies can be enhanced with flavored icings, fillings, and jams, offering a burst of complementary tastes to the classic sugar base.

9. **Tips and Techniques for Decorating:**

• The chapter provides step-by-step guides to decorating sugar cookies, from outlining and flooding with icing to creating intricate designs using piping techniques.

10. **Holiday and Themed Sugar Cookies:**

• Sugar cookies are a staple for holidays and special occasions. Learn how to create themed cookies for events like Christmas, Valentine's Day, birthdays, and more.

11. **Creating Edible Art:**

• Sugar cookies can be transformed into edible art, resembling intricate designs, floral arrangements, or even scenes from nature. This chapter delves into advanced decorating techniques for those looking to elevate their cookie artistry.

12. **Storing and Gifting:**

• Discover how to store sugar cookies to keep them fresh and crisp. Also, learn about creative packaging ideas for gifting these delightful treats.

Sugar cookies are more than just baked goods; they're a form of edible art that lets your imagination run wild. Whether you're a beginner or an experienced decorator, sugar cookies offer a delightful creative outlet that can be shared with loved ones and cherished as edible works of art. As you dive into the world of sugar cookies, you'll find endless inspiration and enjoyment, and you may even discover a new passion for cookie decorating. Happy baking and decorating!

- **Oatmeal Raisin Cookies**

Oatmeal raisin cookies are the wholesome classic of the cookie world. The nutty, hearty flavor of oats combines with the natural sweetness of raisins to create a treat that's both comforting and nutritious. In this chapter, we explore the delightful world of oatmeal raisin cookies, from the perfect texture to ingredient variations and even some tips for making them even more delicious.

1. **The Comfort of Oatmeal Raisin Cookies:**

- Oatmeal raisin cookies are a timeless comfort food. Their hearty, nutty flavor and the natural sweetness of plump raisins make them a favorite choice for a cozy snack or dessert.

2. **Ingredients for Oatmeal Raisin Cookies:**

- Oatmeal raisin cookies are made with a blend of ingredients, each contributing to their distinct flavor and texture:

- **Rolled Oats:** The star ingredient, providing a hearty texture and nutty flavor.

- **Butter:** Offers richness and a buttery taste.

- **Sugar:** A combination of brown and granulated sugar lends sweetness, moisture, and a soft texture.

- **Egg:** Acts as a binder, adding structure and moisture.

- **Vanilla Extract:** Enhances the overall flavor.
- **Flour:** Forms the cookie's structure.
- **Baking Soda:** Provides leavening for a tender, slightly puffy texture.
- **Cinnamon:** Adds warm, comforting spice.
- **Salt:** Balances the sweetness and enhances all the flavors.

3. **Texture Variations:**
- Oatmeal raisin cookies offer versatility in texture. You can customize them to be soft and chewy or slightly crispy. Ingredient ratios and baking times play a significant role in achieving the desired texture.

4. **Ingredient Variations:**
- Explore different ingredient variations such as using old-fashioned oats for a heartier texture or quick oats for a softer one. You can also experiment with adding nuts or spices like nutmeg for unique flavor profiles.

5. **The Science of Oats:**
- Oats contain soluble fiber, which contributes to the cookies' slightly chewy texture. Understanding the difference between types of oats and how they affect the final product is key to mastering oatmeal raisin cookies.

6. **Mixing and Baking Tips:**
- This chapter provides insights into mixing the dough, ensuring that the oats are evenly distributed, and offering guidance on proper baking times to achieve the ideal level of doneness.

7. **Dried Fruit Variations:**

- While raisins are the traditional choice, you can experiment with other dried fruits like cranberries, chopped apricots, or dates to create your signature oatmeal cookie.

8. **Serving and Pairing:**

- Discover creative serving ideas for your oatmeal raisin cookies, from simple milk to gourmet ice cream pairings.

9. **Healthier Oatmeal Raisin Cookies:**

- Learn how to make healthier versions of oatmeal raisin cookies by reducing sugar and butter while incorporating wholesome ingredients like whole wheat flour and honey.

Oatmeal raisin cookies embody the perfect blend of comforting flavors, a touch of nostalgia, and a healthy dose of oat goodness. Whether you prefer them chewy, crispy, or with a unique twist, oatmeal raisin cookies are a delicious journey that caters to both the palate and the soul. As you delve into the world of these cookies, you'll find endless possibilities for customization and enjoy the wholesome goodness they bring to your cookie collection.

- **Peanut Butter Cookies**

Peanut butter cookies are an all-time favorite, known for their rich, nutty flavor and that classic crisscross pattern. In this chapter, we explore the world of peanut butter cookies, from their history and basic ingredients to variations, texture choices, and even some creative ways to enjoy this beloved treat.

1. **The Enduring Appeal of Peanut Butter Cookies:**

- Peanut butter cookies hold a special place in the hearts of many. They're cherished for their robust, nutty flavor and the iconic crisscross pattern made with a fork. This chapter explores the history and charm of peanut butter cookies.

2. **Ingredients for Peanut Butter Cookies:**

- Peanut butter cookies come to life with a handful of key ingredients:
- **Peanut Butter:** The star of the show, it provides the nutty flavor and unique texture.
- **Butter:** Offers richness and helps with tenderness.
- **Sugar:** A combination of granulated and brown sugar provides sweetness and texture.
- **Egg:** Acts as a binder, adding moisture and structure.
- **Vanilla Extract:** Enhances the overall flavor.
- **Flour:** Forms the cookie's structure.
- **Baking Soda:** Provides leavening for a slightly puffy texture.
- **Salt:** Balances the sweetness and highlights the flavors.

3. **Texture Variations:**

- Peanut butter cookies offer versatility in texture. You can customize them to be soft and chewy or slightly crisp. Ingredient ratios and baking times play a significant role in achieving the desired texture.

4. **Ingredient Variations:**

- Experiment with ingredient variations like natural peanut butter for a deeper nutty flavor or chunky peanut butter to add texture. You can also enhance the cookies with the addition of chocolate chips, chopped nuts, or even a hint of spice like cinnamon.

5. **The Science of Peanut Butter:**

- Peanut butter contains both fat and protein, which contribute to the cookies' unique texture and flavor. This chapter explains the importance of selecting the right type of peanut butter and provides insights into achieving the desired consistency.

6. **Mixing and Baking Tips:**

- This chapter offers guidance on mixing the dough to ensure that the peanut butter is evenly incorporated. Proper baking times are also discussed to achieve the perfect balance of tenderness and flavor.

7. **Creative Peanut Butter Cookie Creations:**

- Discover imaginative ways to take your peanut butter cookies to the next level by sandwiching them with fillings, drizzling them with chocolate, or creating thumbprint cookies with a variety of toppings.

8. **Serving and Pairing:**

- Find inspiration for serving your peanut butter cookies, whether as an accompaniment to a glass of milk or paired with gourmet ice cream flavors.

9. **Healthier Peanut Butter Cookies:**

- Learn how to make healthier versions of peanut butter cookies by reducing sugar and butter while incorporating wholesome ingredients like whole wheat flour and oats.

Peanut butter cookies are more than a delicious treat; they're a source of nostalgia and a symbol of comfort. Whether you prefer them soft, crunchy, or with an inventive twist, peanut butter cookies offer endless possibilities for customization. As you delve into the world of these cookies, you'll discover the magic of peanut butter and its ability to transform a simple recipe into a beloved classic.

- **Snickerdoodles**

Snickerdoodles are the delightful, sugar-coated cinnamon cookies that offer a perfect combination of sweetness and warmth. In this chapter, we'll explore the world of Snickerdoodles, from their origins to the key ingredients, the science behind their unique texture, and ways to get creative with this beloved classic.

1. **The Timeless Charm of Snickerdoodles:**

- Snickerdoodles hold a special place in the world of cookies with their simple yet enticing combination of sugar and cinnamon. Their origins and enduring popularity are explored in this chapter.

2. **Ingredients for Snickerdoodles:**

- Snickerdoodles rely on a handful of essential ingredients:
- **Butter:** Adds richness and flavor.
- **Sugar:** Provides sweetness and aids in the cookie's texture.

- **Eggs:** Act as binders, adding moisture and structure.

- **Vanilla Extract:** Enhances the overall flavor.

- **Flour:** Forms the cookie's structure.

- **Cream of Tartar:** A unique ingredient that contributes to the cookie's distinct texture and tangy flavor.

- **Baking Soda:** Provides leavening for a puffy yet slightly chewy texture.

- **Salt:** Balances the sweetness and enhances the cookie's overall taste.

3. **Texture Variations:**

- Snickerdoodles offer versatility in texture. You can customize them to be soft and chewy or slightly crispy by adjusting ingredient ratios and baking times.

4. **Cinnamon Sugar Coating:**

- The iconic outer layer of Snickerdoodles is a combination of cinnamon and sugar, which provides a delightful crunch and warmth to these cookies.

5. **The Science of Cream of Tartar:**

- Cream of tartar is a key ingredient in Snickerdoodles that affects their texture and provides a subtle tang. This chapter delves into the role of cream of tartar in achieving the cookie's unique characteristics.

6. **Mixing and Baking Tips:**

- This chapter provides guidance on mixing the dough to ensure proper incorporation of ingredients. It also offers insights into the ideal baking times to achieve that perfect balance of tenderness and flavor.

7. **Creative Variations:**

- Discover inventive ways to elevate your Snickerdoodles, such as sandwiching them with fillings, incorporating additional spices like nutmeg, or experimenting with flavored sugars for the coating.

8. **Serving and Pairing:**

- Find inspiration for serving your Snickerdoodles, whether as an accompaniment to a cupful of tea or coffee or paired with your favorite ice cream.

9. **Healthier Snickerdoodles:**

- Learn how to make healthier versions of Snickerdoodles by reducing sugar and butter while incorporating wholesome ingredients like whole wheat flour and alternative sweeteners.

Snickerdoodles are a beloved classic that brings a touch of warmth and nostalgia to every bite. Whether you prefer them soft, crispy, or with an innovative twist, Snickerdoodles offer endless possibilities for customization and experimentation. As you explore the world of these cookies, you'll uncover the magic of cinnamon and cream of tartar, which transforms a simple recipe into a cherished favorite.

CHAPTER 5
COOKIE TROUBLESHOOTING

- **Common Baking Mistakes**

Baking, while a delightful and rewarding culinary adventure, can sometimes be fraught with pitfalls that even the most experienced bakers encounter. This chapter is your guide to recognizing and avoiding common baking mistakes, ensuring that your journey in the world of cookies and other baked goods is filled with delicious success.

1. **Inaccurate Measurements:**

- One of the most fundamental mistakes in baking is inaccurate measurements. Using too much or too little of an ingredient can drastically affect the outcome of your cookies. Invest in proper measuring tools, and remember to measure dry ingredients like flour by spooning and leveling.

2. **Incorrect Oven Temperature:**

- Baking at the wrong temperature can lead to cookies that are overdone, underdone, or unevenly baked. Invest in an oven thermometer to ensure your oven is calibrated correctly, and always Heat in advance it to the recommended temperature.

3. **Overmixing the Dough:**

- Overmixing cookie dough can lead to tough, dry cookies. Learn when to stop mixing; for most recipes, mixing until the ingredients are just combined is sufficient. Save the vigorous mixing for bread and cake batters.

4. **Neglecting to Chill the Dough:**

- For some cookie recipes, chilling the dough is crucial. Failing to do so can result in cookies that spread too much during baking. Follow the recipe instructions and don't skip this step when needed.

5. **Not Using Parchment Paper:**

- Baking on bare cookie sheets can lead to cookies that bar and break. Use parchment paper or silicone baking mats to ensure your cookies release easily and maintain their shape.

6. **Overcrowding the Baking Sheet:**

- Overcrowding the baking sheet can cause cookies to merge into one another. Leave enough space between each cookie to allow for spreading during baking. If necessary, bake in multiple batches.

7. **Ignoring the Role of Altitude:**

- Altitude affects baking, particularly for leavened baked goods like cookies. High altitudes can lead to cookies that rise too quickly and then collapse. Adjust your recipes if you live at a high altitude.

8. **Substituting Ingredients Without Understanding:**

- Substituting ingredients without understanding their function can lead to undesirable results. For instance, substituting baking soda for baking powder or using salted butter when unsalted is called for can drastically affect your cookies.

9. **Not Checking Doneness Early Enough:**

- Cookies continue to cook slightly after being removed from the oven due to residual heat. If you wait until your cookies look done in the oven, they may overbake as they cool. Take them out when they are slightly underdone and let them finish on the baking sheet.

10. **Impatience:**

- Baking requires patience. Rushing through the steps or attempting to remove cookies from the baking sheet too soon can lead to cookie disasters. Allow your cookies to cool on the baking sheet for a few minutes before transferring them to a cooling rack.

11. **Skipping Recipe Reading:**

- Skipping over or misinterpreting steps in a recipe can lead to errors. Always read the recipe thoroughly and follow the instructions precisely.

12. **Lack of Experimentation:**

- While precise following of a recipe is essential, some bakers bar to a single recipe without experimenting. Baking is an art, and you can make your cookies unique by tweaking ingredients, textures, and flavors.

13. **Failing to Record Your Experiments:**

- When you do experiment with a recipe, make sure to take notes on what you changed and the results. This helps you learn from your experiences and refine your baking skills.

14. **Not Allowing Cookies to Cool:**

- Cookies need time to cool and set after baking. Attempting to enjoy them while they are still hot can lead to a crumbly mess. Be patient and let them cool before indulging.

15. **Giving Up Too Soon:**

- Baking is a skill that improves with practice. Don't be discouraged by early failures. Learn from your mistakes and keep experimenting; your baking skills will improve over time.

Avoiding these common baking mistakes can help you create cookies that are not only delicious but also beautifully textured and visually appealing. Baking is an art that combines precision and creativity, and by learning from your mistakes, you'll become a confident and skilled baker who can delight in the joy of creating delectable treats.

- **Overcoming Texture Issues**

Texture plays a crucial role in the enjoyment of cookies. Achieving the perfect texture can be a challenge, but with the right knowledge and techniques, you can overcome common texture issues and create cookies that are tender, chewy, crispy, or any texture you desire. In this chapter, we'll explore how to address and overcome texture problems in your cookie-baking adventures.

1. **Overly Dry Cookies:**

- If your cookies turn out dry and crumbly, it may be due to using too much flour or overbaking. Reduce the flour in your recipe and ensure you bake your cookies for a shorter time. You can also add a bit more fat or moisture to the dough, such as extra butter or egg yolk.

2. **Cookies That Spread Too Much:**

- When cookies spread excessively during baking, they often become thin and flat. To combat this issue, try chilling the dough before baking. You can also increase the flour in your recipe and reduce the fat or sugar.

3. **Cakey Cookies:**

- Cakey cookies can be the result of too much flour or too little fat. Adjust your recipe by using less flour and increasing the fat (butter, oil, or shortening). Also, ensure you don't overmix the dough.

4. **Cookies That Are Too Tough or Hard:**

- Tough or hard cookies can be due to overmixing, overbaking, or using too much flour. Reduce mixing time, bake for a shorter period, and decrease the flour in your recipe. You can also add a bit more fat or moisture to soften the cookies.

5. **Cookies That Are Too Chewy:**

- Achieving the perfect level of chewiness can be a challenge. To make cookies less chewy, reduce the sugar and use more fat. You can also experiment with different types of sugar to achieve your desired texture.

6. **Cookies with Gummy Centers:**

- Gummy centers are often caused by underbaking. Ensure that you bake your cookies for the recommended time, and they'll be cooked through and not gummy. Adjusting the ratio of sugar to fat can also help with this issue.

7. **Texture Issues Due to Gluten Formation:**

- Overmixing and excessive gluten formation can lead to undesirable textures. To prevent this, mix your cookie dough just until the ingredients are combined. Consider using cake flour or pastry flour, which has less protein and forms less gluten.

8. **Browning Problems:**

- Achieving the right level of browning is essential for texture and flavor. If your cookies brown too quickly or too slowly, consider adjusting the sugar or fat in your recipe and ensure accurate oven temperature.

9. **Inconsistent Texture in Large Batches:**

- When baking in large batches, achieving consistent texture can be challenging. Rotate your baking sheets, use an oven thermometer, and maintain a consistent cookie size to ensure even baking.

10. **Customizing Texture to Your Liking:**

•   Cookie texture is highly customizable. Learn to adjust your recipes to achieve your preferred level of tenderness, chewiness, or crispness.

11. **Using Proper Mixing Techniques:**

•   The way you mix your cookie dough can significantly impact texture. Learn when to cream, fold, and mix to achieve your desired results.

12. **Using the Right Ingredients:**

•   Choose ingredients that align with your desired texture. For example, use bread flour for chewier cookies or cake flour for softer ones.

Overcoming texture issues in your cookies is a skill that develops with practice. By understanding the factors that influence texture and experimenting with different ingredients and techniques, you can achieve the perfect texture in your cookies, making them a delight for your taste buds and a source of pride in your baking repertoire.

•   **Perfecting Flavor**

Flavor is the heart and soul of your cookies. Perfecting the flavor is about creating a delicious and harmonious taste that resonates with your palate. In this chapter, we'll explore the art and science of flavor in cookie baking, offering insights into ingredient selection, flavor balance, and enhancing the taste of your cookies.

1. **Understanding Ingredient Flavor Profiles:**

•   To perfect the flavor of your cookies, it's essential to understand the flavor profiles of individual ingredients. Ingredients like vanilla, cocoa, spices, and extracts all contribute unique flavors. Experiment with various brands and types to find your preferred taste.

2. **Selecting High-Quality Ingredients:**

- The quality of your ingredients directly impacts the flavor of your cookies. Choose fresh, high-quality ingredients, such as pure vanilla extract, real butter, and premium chocolate. Avoid artificial flavorings when possible.

3. **Balancing Sweetness:**

- Achieving the right level of sweetness is crucial. Experiment with the balance of granulated sugar, brown sugar, and alternative sweeteners to achieve your preferred level of sweetness. Keep in mind that sugar not only sweetens but also contributes to texture and browning.

4. **Harnessing the Power of Salt:**

- Salt is a flavor enhancer that can elevate the taste of your cookies. A pinch of salt not only balances sweetness but also enhances the overall flavor. Experiment with different types of salt (sea salt, kosher salt, etc.) to discover their unique effects on taste.

5. **Spices and Extracts:**

- Spices and extracts can transform your cookies. Explore a variety of spices, such as cinnamon, nutmeg, or cardamom, to add warmth and depth.

Additionally, different extracts like almond, lemon, or mint can impart distinct and exciting flavors to your cookies.

6. **Enhancing Flavor with Mix-Ins:**

- Mix-ins like chocolate chips, nuts, dried fruits, and spices can add complexity and depth to your cookies' flavor. Experiment with different combinations to find your perfect match.

7. **The Role of Leavening Agents:**

- Baking soda and baking powder not only leaven your cookies but also impact their flavor. Baking soda, when not sufficiently neutralized by acid, can result in a bitter taste. Baking powder may have a slight metallic taste if too much is used. Understand the role of leavening agents to avoid these flavor issues.

8. **Controlling Flavor with Temperature:**

- The temperature at which you bake your cookies can affect their flavor. Higher temperatures often lead to cookies with a more complex flavor, while lower temperatures can result in cookies that taste sweeter and more buttery. Experiment with different temperatures to find the flavor profile you prefer.

9. **Flavor Evolution:**

- Consider that the flavor of some cookies may improve and evolve over time. Storing your cookies in an airtight container allows the flavors to meld and mature, potentially resulting in a richer taste.

10. **Pairing Flavors:**

- Complementary flavors can elevate the taste of your cookies. Think about flavor pairings like chocolate and orange, cinnamon and apple, or nutmeg and pear. These combinations can create a symphony of tastes.

11. **Recording Your Experiments:**

- Keep a record of your flavor experiments, noting the ingredients, proportions, and techniques you used. This helps you replicate your successes and avoid repeating any flavor missteps.

Perfecting the flavor of your cookies is a delightful journey in creativity and palate exploration. By understanding the flavors of your ingredients, experimenting with various combinations, and balancing sweetness and spice, you can craft cookies that not only look inviting but also captivate your taste buds with their delicious, harmonious taste.

CHAPTER 6
CLASSIC COOKIE CREATIONS

1. Peanut Butter Cookies

Ingredients:

- one cupful (two bars) unsalted butter, softened
- one cupful creamy peanut butter
- one cupful granulated sugar
- one cupful brown sugar, packed
- two large eggs
- one teaspoonful pure vanilla extract
- two half cupful all-purpose flour

- one half teaspoons baking soda
- half teaspoonful salt

Instructions:

1. Heat in advance your oven to 350°F, One hundred and Seventy Five degrees Celsius

2. In a large mixing bowl, cream together the butter, peanut butter, granulated sugar, and brown sugar until light and fluffy.

3. Beat in the eggs one at a time, then stir in the vanilla.

4. In a separate bowl, combine the flour, baking soda, and salt. Gradually add the dry ingredients to the wet ingredients and mix until just combined.

5. Drop rounded tablespoonful of dough onto ungreased baking sheets.

6. Use a fork to create the classic crisscross pattern on the cookies.

7. Bake for ten-twelve minutes, or until the edges are golden.

8. Allow cookies to cool on the baking sheets for a few minutes before transferring them to a wire rack to cool completely.

Duration: twenty two minutes

Nutrients (per portion):

- Caloric content: 160
- Fatty acid: 8g
- Carb content: 19g
- Amino content: 3g

2. Sugar Cookies

Ingredients:

- one cupful (two bars) unsalted butter, softened
- one cupful granulated sugar
- two large eggs
- one teaspoonful pure vanilla extract
- three cupful all-purpose flour
- half teaspoonful baking powder
- half teaspoonful salt

Instructions:

1. Heat in advance your oven to 350°F, One hundred and Seventy Five degrees Celsius

2. In a large mixing bowl, cream together the butter and granulated sugar until light and fluffy.

3. Beat in the eggs one at a time, then stir in the vanilla.

4. In a separate bowl, combine the flour, baking powder, and salt. Gradually add the dry ingredients to the wet ingredients and mix until just combined.

5. Roll out the dough on a floured surface to your desired thickness, and use cookie cutters to create shapes.

6. Place cookies on ungreased baking sheets.

7. Bake for eight-ten minutes, or until the edges are lightly golden.

8. Allow cookies to cool on the baking sheets for a few minutes before transferring them to a wire rack to cool completely.

Duration: eighteen minutes

Nutrients (per portion):

- Caloric content: 120
- Fatty acid: 5g
- Carb content: eighteen grams
- Amino content: 2g

3. Snickerdoodles

Ingredients:

- one cupful (two bars) unsalted butter, softened
- one half cupful granulated sugar
- two large eggs
- two three-fourth cupful all-purpose flour
- two teaspoons cream of tartar
- one teaspoonful baking soda
- half teaspoonful salt

For Rolling:

- two tablespoonful granulated sugar
- two teaspoons ground cinnamon

Instructions:

1. Heat in advance your oven to 400°F (200°C).

2. In a large mixing bowl, cream together the butter and one half cupful of sugar until light and fluffy.

3. Beat in the eggs one at a time.

4. In a separate bowl, combine the flour, cream of tartar, baking soda, and salt. Gradually add the dry ingredients to the wet ingredients and mix until just combined.

5. In a small bowl, mix together the remaining two tablespoonful of sugar and ground cinnamon.

6. Shape the dough into one-inch balls and roll them in the cinnamon-sugar mixture.

7. Place the coated dough balls on ungreased baking sheets.

8. Bake for eight-ten minutes, or until the edges are golden but the centers are still soft.

9. Allow cookies to cool on the baking sheets for a few minutes before transferring them to a wire rack to cool completely.

Duration: eighteen minutes

Nutrients (per portion):

- Caloric content: 120

- Fatty acid: 5g

- Carb content: eighteen grams

- Amino content: 2g

4. Chocolate Crinkle Cookies

Ingredients:

- half cupful unsweetened cocoa powder
- one cupful granulated sugar
- one-fourth cupful vegetable oil
- two large eggs
- one teaspoonful pure vanilla extract
- one cupful all-purpose flour
- one teaspoonful baking powder
- half teaspoonful salt
- half cupful powdered sugar for rolling

Instructions:

1. In a medium mixing bowl, whisk together the cocoa powder, granulated sugar, and vegetable oil until well combined.

2. Beat in the eggs one at a time, then stir in the vanilla.

3. In a separate bowl, combine the flour, baking powder, and salt. Gradually add the dry ingredients to the wet ingredients and mix until just combined.

4. Cover the dough and chill it in the refrigerator for at least four hours or overnight.

5. Heat in advance your oven to 350°F, One hundred and Seventy Five degrees Celsius

6. Shape the dough into one-inch balls, roll them in powdered sugar, and place them on ungreased baking sheets.

7. Bake for ten-twelve minutes, or until the cookies have cracked and are set.

8. Allow cookies to cool on the baking sheets for a few minutes before transferring them to a wire rack to cool completely.

Duration: twenty two minutes

Nutrients (per portion):

- Caloric content: 80
- Fatty acid: 3g
- Carb content: 12g
- Amino content: 1g

5. Gingerbread crunch Cookies

Ingredients:

- three cupful all-purpose flour
- one half teaspoons ground ginger
- one half teaspoons ground cinnamon
- half teaspoonful ground cloves
- half teaspoonful baking soda
- half teaspoonful salt
- half cupful (one bar) unsalted butter, softened
- half cupful granulated sugar

- one large egg
- half cupful molasses

Instructions:

1. In a medium bowl, whisk together the flour, ginger, cinnamon, cloves, baking soda, and salt.

2. In a separate large mixing bowl, cream together the butter and granulated sugar until light and fluffy.

3. Beat in the egg and molasses.

4. Gradually add the dry ingredients to the wet ingredients and mix until just combined.

5. Cover the dough and chill it in the refrigerator for at least one hour.

6. Heat in advance your oven to 350°F, One hundred and Seventy Five degrees Celsius

7. Roll out the dough on a floured surface to your desired thickness and use cookie cutters to create shapes.

8. Place cookies on ungreased baking sheets.

9. Bake for eight-ten minutes, or until the edges are set.

10. Allow cookies to cool on the baking sheets for a few minutes before transferring them to a wire rack to cool completely.

Duration: eighteen minutes

Nutrients (per portion):

- Caloric content: thousand

- Fatty acid: 2g
- Carb content: 20g
- Amino content: 2g

6. Classic Shortbread Cookies

Ingredients:

- one cupful (two bars) unsalted butter, softened
- half cupful granulated sugar
- two cupful all-purpose flour
- one-fourth teaspoonful salt

Instructions:

1. Heat in advance your oven to 350°F, One hundred and Seventy Five degrees Celsius

2. In a large mixing bowl, cream together the butter and granulated sugar until smooth and creamy.

3. In a separate bowl, combine the flour and salt. Gradually add the dry ingredients to the wet ingredients and mix until just combined.

4. Roll the dough into a half-inch thick rectangle and cut into your desired shapes.

5. Place cookies on an ungreased baking sheet.

6. Bake for twelve-fifteen minutes, or until the edges are lightly golden.

7. Allow cookies to cool on the baking sheet for a few minutes before transferring them to a wire rack to cool completely.

Duration: fifteen minutes

Nutrients (per portion):

- Caloric content: thousand
- Fatty acid: 7g
- Carb content: 9g
- Amino content: 1g

7. Classic Snickerdoodles

Ingredients:

- half cupful (one bar) unsalted butter, softened
- one cupful granulated sugar
- one large egg
- one teaspoonful pure vanilla extract
- one half cupful all-purpose flour
- one-fourth teaspoonful cream of tartar
- one-fourth teaspoonful baking soda
- one-fourth teaspoonful salt

For Rolling:

- two tablespoonful granulated sugar
- one teaspoonful ground cinnamon

Instructions:

1. Heat in advance your oven to 375°F (190°C).

2. In a large mixing bowl, cream together the butter and one cupful of sugar until light and fluffy.

3. Beat in the egg and vanilla.

4. In a separate bowl, combine the flour, cream of tartar, baking soda, and salt. Gradually add the dry ingredients to the wet ingredients and mix until just combined.

5. In a small bowl, mix together the remaining two tablespoonful of sugar and ground cinnamon.

6. Shape the dough into one-inch balls, roll them in the cinnamon-sugar mixture, and place them on an ungreased baking sheet.

7. Bake for ten-twelve minutes, or until the edges are golden but the centers are still soft.

8. Allow cookies to cool on the baking sheet for a few minutes before transferring them to a wire rack to cool completely.

Duration: twenty two minutes

Nutrients (per portion):

- Caloric content: 90
- Fatty acid: 4g
- Carb content: 13g
- Amino content: 1g

8. Classic Thumbprint Cookies

Ingredients:

- one cupful (two bars) unsalted butter, softened
- two-third cupful granulated sugar
- two large egg yolks
- one teaspoonful pure vanilla extract
- two cupful all-purpose flour
- one-fourth teaspoonful salt
- half cupful fruit jam or preserves (your choice)

Instructions:

1. Heat in advance your oven to 350°F, One hundred and Seventy Five degrees Celsius

2. In a large mixing bowl, cream together the butter and sugar until light and fluffy.

3. Beat in the egg yolks and vanilla.

4. In a separate bowl, combine the flour and salt. Gradually add the dry ingredients to the wet ingredients and mix until just combined.

5. Roll the dough into one-inch balls and place them on an ungreased baking sheet.

6. Use your thumb to create an indentation in the center of each cookie.

7. Fill each indentation with a small amount of fruit jam or preserves.

8. Bake for twelve-fifteen minutes, or until the edges are lightly golden.

9. Allow cookies to cool on the baking sheet for a few minutes before transferring them to a wire rack to cool completely.

Duration: fifteen minutes

Nutrients (per portion):

- Caloric content: 120
- Fatty acid: 6g
- Carb content: 15g
- Amino content: 1g

9. Classic Anzac Biscuits (Cookies)

Ingredients:

- one cupful rolled oats
- one cupful all-purpose flour
- one cupful desiccated coconut
- half cupful granulated sugar
- half cupful brown sugar, packed
- half cupful (one bar) unsalted butter
- two tablespoonful golden syrup (or light corn syrup)
- half teaspoonful baking soda
- two tablespoonful hot water

Instructions:

1. Heat in advance your oven to 325°F (160°C).

2. In a large mixing bowl, combine the rolled oats, flour, coconut, granulated sugar, and brown sugar.

3. In a saucepan, melt the butter and golden syrup over low heat. In a small bowl, dissolve the baking soda in the hot water and add it to the butter mixture.

4. Pour the liquid mixture into the dry ingredients and stir until well combined.

5. Drop rounded tablespoonful of dough onto a lined baking sheet and flatten them slightly with a fork.

6. Bake for twelve-fifteen minutes, or until the cookies are golden.

7. Allow cookies to cool on the baking sheet for a few minutes before transferring them to a wire rack to cool completely.

Duration: fifteen minutes

Nutrients (per portion):

- Caloric content: one hundred ten
- Fatty acid: 5g
- Carb content: 16g
- Amino content: 1g

10. Classic Peanut Butter Blossom Cookies

Ingredients:

- half cupful (one bar) unsalted butter, softened

- half cupful creamy peanut butter
- half cupful granulated sugar
- half cupful brown sugar, packed
- one large egg
- one teaspoonful pure vanilla extract
- one three-fourth cupful all-purpose flour
- one teaspoonful baking soda
- half teaspoonful salt
- 36 chocolate kisses, unwrapped

Instructions:

1. Heat in advance your oven to 375°F (190°C).

2. In a large mixing bowl, cream together the butter, peanut butter, granulated sugar, and brown sugar until light and fluffy.

3. Beat in the egg and vanilla.

4. In a separate bowl, combine the flour, baking soda, and salt. Gradually add the dry ingredients to the wet ingredients and mix until just combined.

5. Shape the dough into one-inch balls and place them on an ungreased baking sheet.

6. Bake for eight-ten minutes, or until the edges are golden.

7. As soon as you remove the cookies from the oven, press a chocolate kiss into the center of each cookie.

8. Allow cookies to cool on the baking sheet for a few minutes before transferring them to a wire rack to cool completely.

Duration: eighteen minutes

Nutrients (per portion):

- Caloric content: thousand
- Fatty acid: 4g
- Carb content: 15g
- Amino content: 2g

11. Classic Almond Biscotti

Ingredients:

- half cupful (one bar) unsalted butter, softened
- one cupful granulated sugar
- three large eggs
- one teaspoonful pure almond extract
- two three-fourth cupful all-purpose flour
- one half teaspoons baking powder
- one-fourth teaspoonful salt
- one cupful whole almonds (with skins)

Instructions:

1. Heat in advance your oven to 350°F, One hundred and Seventy Five degrees Celsius

2. In a large mixing bowl, cream together the butter and sugar until light and fluffy.

3. Beat in the eggs one at a time, then stir in the almond extract.

4. In a separate bowl, combine the flour, baking powder, and salt. Gradually add the dry ingredients to the wet ingredients and mix until just combined.

5. Stir in the whole almonds.

6. Divide the dough in half and shape each portion into a log about twelve inches long and two inches wide. Place the logs on a baking sheet.

7. Bake for 30-thirty five minutes, or until the logs are lightly golden and firm to the touch.

8. Remove the logs from the oven and let them cool for ten minutes. Reduce the oven temperature to 325°F (160°C).

9. Slice the logs into half-inch thick slices. Lay the slices on their sides on the baking sheet.

10. Bake for an additional ten-fifteen minutes, or until the biscotti are golden and crisp.

11. Allow cookies to cool on the baking sheet for a few minutes before transferring them to a wire rack to cool completely.

Duration: forty five minutes

Nutrients (per portion):

- Caloric content: 120

- Fatty acid: 6g

- Carb content: 15g
- Amino content: 3g

12. Classic Coconut Macaroons

Ingredients:

- four large egg whites
- one-fourth cupful granulated sugar
- half teaspoonful pure vanilla extract
- 1/8 teaspoonful salt
- three cupful sweetened shredded coconut

Instructions:

1. Heat in advance your oven to 350°F, One hundred and Seventy Five degrees Celsius

2. In a large mixing bowl, beat the egg whites until stiff peaks form.

3. Gradually add the sugar, vanilla extract, and salt, continuing to beat until well combined.

4. Gently fold in the shredded coconut.

5. Drop rounded tablespoonful of the mixture onto a parchment paper-lined baking sheet.

6. Bake for 15-eighteen minutes, or until the macaroons are lightly golden on the outside.

7. Allow cookies to cool on the baking sheet for a few minutes before transferring them to a wire rack to cool completely.

Duration: eighteen minutes

Nutrients (per portion):

- Caloric content: 80
- Fatty acid: 5g
- Carb content: 7g
- Amino content: 1g

13. Classic Linzer Cookies

Ingredients:

- one cupful (two bars) unsalted butter, softened
- half cupful granulated sugar
- two large egg yolks
- two teaspoons pure vanilla extract
- two cupful all-purpose flour
- half teaspoonful ground cinnamon
- one-fourth teaspoonful salt
- half cupful raspberry or apricot jam
- Confectioners' sugar for dusting

Instructions:

1. In a large mixing bowl, cream together the butter and granulated sugar until light and fluffy.

2. Beat in the egg yolks and vanilla.

3. In a separate bowl, combine the flour, ground cinnamon, and salt. Gradually add the dry ingredients to the wet ingredients and mix until just combined.

4. Divide the dough in half and shape each portion into a disk. Wrap them in plastic wrap and chill in the refrigerator for at least 30 minutes.

5. Heat in advance your oven to 350°F, One hundred and Seventy Five degrees Celsius

6. Roll out one of the dough disks on a floured surface to about 1/eight-inch thickness. Cut out cookies using a round cookie cutter and cut out the centers of half of the cookies using a smaller shape (such as a heart).

7. Place the cookies on a baking sheet lined with parchment paper and bake for ten-twelve minutes, or until they are lightly golden.

8. Allow cookies to cool on the baking sheet for a few minutes before transferring them to a wire rack to cool completely.

9. Heat the jam in a small saucepan until it becomes spreadable.

10. Spread a thin layer of jam on the solid cookies and then top each with a cutout cookie.

11. Dust the tops of the cookies with confectioners' sugar.

Duration: twelve minutes

Nutrients (per portion):

- Caloric content: 120

- Fatty acid: 6g

- Carb content: 15g

- Amino content: 1g

14. Classic Biscuit (Cookie) Sandwiches

Ingredients:

- one cupful (two bars) unsalted butter, softened

- half cupful granulated sugar

- two cupful all-purpose flour

- half teaspoonful salt

- Jam or chocolate spread for filling

Instructions:

1. Heat in advance your oven to 350°F, One hundred and Seventy Five degrees Celsius

2. In a large mixing bowl, cream together the butter and sugar until light and fluffy.

3. In a separate bowl, combine the flour and salt. Gradually add the dry ingredients to the wet ingredients and mix until just combined.

4. Roll out the dough on a floured surface to about 1/4-inch thickness.

5. Cut out cookies using a round or shaped cookie cutter.

6. Place the cookies on a baking sheet lined with parchment paper and bake for ten-twelve minutes, or until they are lightly golden.

7. Allow cookies to cool on the baking sheet for a few minutes before transferring them to a wire rack to cool completely.

8. Once the cookies have cooled, spread jam or chocolate spread on the flat side of one cookie and sandwich it with another.

Duration: twelve minutes

Nutrients (per portion):

- Caloric content: 90

- Fatty acid: 5g

- Carb content: ten grams

- Amino content: 1g

15. Classic Oatmeal bars

Ingredients:

- one cupful (two bars) unsalted butter, softened

- one cupful granulated sugar

- one cupful brown sugar, packed

- two large eggs

- one teaspoonful pure vanilla extract

- one half cupful all-purpose flour

- one teaspoonful baking soda

- one teaspoonful ground cinnamon
- half teaspoonful salt
- three cupful old-fashioned oats
- one cupful raisins

Instructions:

1. Heat in advance the oven to 350°F, One hundred and Seventy Five degrees Celsius

2. In a large mixing bowl, cream the butter, granulated sugar, and brown sugar together.

3. Beat in the eggs and vanilla.

4. In a separate bowl, whisk together the flour, baking soda, cinnamon, and salt. Gradually add this dry mixture to the wet mixture.

5. Stir in the oats and raisins.

6. Drop rounded tablespoonful of dough onto ungreased baking sheets.

7. Bake for ten-twelve minutes or until the edges are golden brown. Cool on wire racks.

Yield: Approximately 36 cookies

Duration: ten-twelve minutes per batch

Estimated Calories per Cookie: thousand-120 calories

CHAPTER 7
FLAVORFUL VARIATIONS

16. Apricot Thumbprint Cookies

Ingredients:

- one cupful (two bars) unsalted butter, softened
- half cupful granulated sugar
- two large egg yolks
- two teaspoonful vanilla extract
- two half cupful all-purpose flour
- one-fourth teaspoonful salt

- half cupful apricot preserves

Instructions:

1. Turn the oven temperature up to three hundred and seventy five degrees Fahrenheit (one hundred and eighty five degrees Celsius).

2. Butter and granulated sugar should be creamed together in a large basin.

3. Egg yolks and vanilla essence should be beaten in.

4. Flour and salt should be mixed separately. Mix this up with the butter slowly.

5. Roll the dough into one-inch balls and arrange them on baking pans lined with parchment paper.

6. Use your thumb or the back of a spoon to press down on the centre of each biscuit.

7. Place a dollop of apricot preserves in each depression.

8. Bake for 12–fifteen minutes, or until the edges are just beginning to turn brown.

Duration: twelve-fifteen minutes

Nutrients (per portion, makes about thirty-six cookies):

- Caloric content: Hundred
- Fatty acid: five grams
- Carb content: thirteen grams
- Amino content: one gram

17. Gingersnap Cookies

Ingredients:

- one cupful (two bars) unsalted butter, softened
- one half cupful granulated sugar
- two large eggs
- half cupful molasses
- four cupful all-purpose flour
- two teaspoonful baking soda
- half teaspoonful salt
- one teaspoonful ground cinnamon
- one teaspoonful ground ginger
- half teaspoonful ground cloves
- Granulated sugar for rolling

Instructions:

1. Turn the oven temperature up to three hundred and seventy five degrees Fahrenheit (one hundred and eighty five degrees Celsius).

2. Butter and half a cupful of granulated sugar should be creamed together in a large bowl.

3. Add the eggs and molasses and mix well.

4. Mix the dry ingredients (flour, baking soda, salt, and spices) in a separate basin. Mix this up with the butter slowly.

5. Roll the dough into balls about an inch in diameter and coat them with sugar.

6. You should bake the cookies on parchment paper.

7. Put in the oven for ten–twelve minutes.

Duration: ten-twelve minutes

Nutrients (per portion, makes about forty-eight cookies):

- Caloric content: one-thirty
- Fatty acid: five grams
- Carb content: twenty grams
- Amino content: two grams

18. Coconut Macaroons

Ingredients:

- four cupful sweetened shredded coconut
- half cupful granulated sugar
- four large egg whites
- one teaspoonful almond extract
- one-fourth teaspoonful salt
- half cupful semisweet chocolate chips (optional)

Instructions:

1. Turn the oven temperature up to three hundred and seventy five degrees Fahrenheit (one hundred and eighty five degrees Celsius).

2. Shredded coconut, white sugar, egg whites, almond essence, and salt are mixed in a bowl.

3. Spoonful of the dough should be placed on baking pans covered with parchment paper.

4. Cook for 15–20 minutes, or until the macaroons are just beginning to turn golden.

5. If chocolate coating is required, chocolate chips may be melted and used to drizzle or dip the macaroons.

Duration: fifteen-twenty minutes

Nutrients (per portion, makes about twenty-four macaroons without chocolate):

- Caloric content: one-thirty
- Fatty acid: seven grams
- Carb content: fifteen grams
- Amino content: one gram

19. Pecan Praline Cookies

Ingredients:

- one cupful (two bars) unsalted butter, softened
- one cupful brown sugar
- one large egg

- two cupful all-purpose flour
- half teaspoonful baking powder
- one-fourth teaspoonful salt
- one cupful chopped pecans
- one teaspoonful vanilla extract

Instructions:

1. Turn the oven temperature up to three hundred and seventy five degrees Fahrenheit (one hundred and eighty five degrees Celsius).

2. Butter and brown sugar should be creamed together in a large bowl.

3. Add the egg and vanilla and mix well.

4. Flour, baking powder, and salt should be mixed together in a separate basin. Mix this up with the butter slowly.

5. Blend in some chopped pecans.

6. Spoonful of cookie dough are dropped onto baking pans coated with paper.

7. Put in the oven for ten–twelve minutes.

Duration: ten-twelve minutes

Nutrients (per portion, makes about thirty-six cookies):

- Caloric content: one-ten
- Fatty acid: seven grams
- Carb content: 1one gram
- Amino content: one gram

20. Anise Pizzelles

Ingredients:

- four large eggs
- one cupful granulated sugar
- two teaspoonful anise extract
- one three-fourth cupful all-purpose flour
- two teaspoonful baking powder
- half cupful (one bar) unsalted butter, melted
- Powdered sugar for dusting

Instructions:

1. To make pizzelles, Heat in advance an appropriate appliance.
2. Eggs and white sugar should be mixed well in a big bowl.
3. Adding the anise essence and mixing it up.
4. Flour and baking powder should be mixed together in a separate basin. Add this to the egg mixture gradually.
5. Butter should be melted and then stirred in.
6. Spoonful of batter are dropped onto the hot pizzelle iron, and the iron is left to cook for as long as the manufacturer specifies (typically about 30 seconds).
7. Take the pizzelles out of the oven and place them on a cooling rack.
8. Serve with a dusting of powdered sugar.

Duration: Varies based on the pizzelle iron

Nutrients (per portion, makes about twenty-four pizzelles):

- Caloric content: one-ten
- Fatty acid: four grams
- Carb content: sixteen grams
- Amino content: two grams

21. Sugar Cookies

Ingredients:

- one cupful (two bars) unsalted butter, softened
- one half cupful granulated sugar
- two large eggs
- one teaspoonful vanilla extract
- three half cupful all-purpose flour
- two teaspoonful baking powder
- half teaspoonful salt

Instructions:

1. Softened butter and sugar should be creamed together in a large bowl until pale and fluffy.

2. Mix in the egg and vanilla extract.

3. Flour, baking powder, and salt should be mixed together in a separate basin.

4. Mix the dry ingredients into the liquid mixture gradually until everything is mixed.

5. Make two discs with the dough and cover them individually in plastic. Put in the fridge and let it chill for at least an hour.

6. Turn the oven temperature up to three hundred and seventy five degrees Fahrenheit (one hundred and eighty five degrees Celsius).

7. On a floured surface, roll out the dough to the appropriate thickness (approximately one-fourth inch is typical). Use cookie cutters to make shapes for the holidays.

8. Bake the cookies for eight to ten minutes, or until they are just beginning to turn golden around the edges, on a baking sheet lined with parchment paper.

9. Sprinkle with sugar or frosting after they have cooled on a wire rack.

Duration: eight-ten minutes

Nutrients (per portion, makes about twenty-four cookies):

- Caloric content: sixteen0
- Fatty acid: seven grams
- Carb content: 2three grams
- Amino content: two grams

22. Gingerbread Cookies

Ingredients:

- three cupful all-purpose flour
- one half teaspoonful ground ginger

- one half teaspoonful ground cinnamon
- one-fourth teaspoonful ground cloves
- half teaspoonful baking soda
- half cupful unsalted butter, softened
- half cupful brown sugar
- one large egg
- half cupful molasses
- one teaspoonful vanilla extract

Instructions:

1. Flour, spices, and baking soda should be mixed together in a bowl.

2. Butter and sugar should be beaten till light and airy in a separate basin. Stir in the beaten egg, molasses, and vanilla. Blend well.

3. To make a dough, slowly incorporate the dry ingredients into the liquid.

4. The dough should be chilled in the fridge for at least one hour after being divided into two discs, wrapped in plastic.

5. Turn the oven temperature up to three hundred and seventy five degrees Fahrenheit (one hundred and eighty five degrees Celsius).

6. Cut out gingerbread men by rolling out the dough.

7. Bake for eight to ten minutes on a baking sheet coated with parchment paper.

8. Put frosting on when it has cooled down.

Duration: eight-ten minutes

Nutrients (per portion, makes about twenty-four cookies):

- Caloric content: one-fifty
- Fatty acid: five grams
- Carb content: twenty five grams
- Amino content: two grams

23. Crispy Chocolate Chip Cookies

Ingredients:

- one cupful (two bars) unsalted butter, softened
- three-fourth cupful granulated sugar
- three-fourth cupful brown sugar
- two large eggs
- one teaspoonful vanilla extract
- two one-fourth cupful all-purpose flour
- one teaspoonful baking soda
- half teaspoonful salt
- two cupful semisweet chocolate chips

Instructions:

1. It is recommended that the oven be Heat in advanceed at three hundred and seventy five degrees Fahrenheit (190 degrees Celsius).

2. Cream the butter, white sugar, and brown sugar together in a large bowl.

3. Mix in the vanilla extract after each egg has been beaten in.

4. Flour, baking powder, and salt should be mixed together in a separate basin. Slowly incorporate this into the butter mixture before folding in the chocolate chunks.

5. Spoonful of cookie dough are placed on baking pans that have not been buttered.

6. Ten to twelve minutes should be enough time to get a light golden colour on the edges.

7. Wait a few minutes for cooling on the baking sheet, then move to wire racks to finish cooling.

Duration: ten-twelve minutes

Nutrients (per portion, makes about thirty-six cookies):

- Caloric content: one-fifty
- Fatty acid: seven grams
- Carb content: twenty grams
- Amino content: two grams

24. Snickerdoodle Cookies

Ingredients:

- one cupful (two bars) unsalted butter, softened
- one half cupful granulated sugar
- two large eggs
- two three-fourth cupful all-purpose flour
- two teaspoonful cream of tartar

- one teaspoonful baking soda
- one-fourth teaspoonful salt
- two tablespoonful granulated sugar
- two teaspoonful ground cinnamon

Instructions:

1. Turn the oven temperature up to three hundred and seventy five degrees Fahrenheit (one hundred and eighty five degrees Celsius).

2. Butter and half a cupful of sugar should be creamed together in a large basin.

3. Add the eggs one at a time and mix well.

4. Flour, cream of tartar, baking soda, and salt should be combined in a separate basin and whisked together.

5. Slowly incorporate the dry ingredients into the liquid.

6. Two teaspoons of sugar and the cinnamon should be mixed together in a separate basin.

7. Form the dough into balls, coat them in the cinnamon-sugar, and set them on baking pans that have not been oiled.

8. If you want golden edges, bake for another minute or two.

Duration: eight-ten minutes

Nutrients (per portion, makes about thirty-six cookies):

- Caloric content: one-twenty
- Fatty acid: five grams

- Carb content: eighteen grams
- Amino content: one gram

25. Peanut Butter Blossoms

Ingredients:

- half cupful (one bar) unsalted butter, softened
- half cupful creamy peanut butter
- half cupful granulated sugar
- half cupful brown sugar
- one large egg
- one one-fourth cupful all-purpose flour
- three-fourth teaspoonful baking soda
- half teaspoonful salt
- thirty-six chocolate Hershey's Kisses, unwrapped

Instructions:

1. It is recommended that the oven be Heat in advanceed at three hundred and seventy five degrees Fahrenheit (190 degrees Celsius).

2. Butter, peanut butter, white sugar, and brown sugar are creamed together in a large basin.

3. Whisk in the egg.

4. Separately, combine the flour, baking powder, and salt in a bowl and mix. Slowly incorporate this into the peanut butter.

5. Roll the dough into balls about an inch in diameter and coat them with sugar.

6. Put them on pans without any oil and bake them for eight-ten minutes.

7. Put a Hershey's Kiss in the middle of each cookie as soon as they come out of the oven.

Duration: eight-ten minutes

Nutrients (per portion, makes about thirty-six cookies):

- Caloric content: 90

- Fatty acid: four grams

- Carb content: 1one gram

- Amino content: two grams

26. Oatmeal Raisin Cookies

Ingredients:

- one cupful (two bars) unsalted butter, softened

- one cupful granulated sugar

- one cupful brown sugar

- two large eggs

- one teaspoonful vanilla extract

- two cupful all-purpose flour

- one teaspoonful baking soda

- one teaspoonful ground cinnamon

- half teaspoonful salt

- three cupful old-fashioned rolled oats
- one cupful raisins

Instructions:

1. Turn the oven temperature up to three hundred and seventy five degrees Fahrenheit (one hundred and eighty five degrees Celsius).

2. Cream the butter, white sugar, and brown sugar together in a large bowl.

3. Mix in the vanilla extract after each egg has been beaten in.

4. The flour, baking soda, cinnamon, and salt should be mixed together in a separate basin. Mix this up with the butter slowly.

5. Add the oats and raisins and mix well.

6. Place dough by the spoonful on baking sheets that have not been oiled.

7. Ten to twelve minutes in the oven should get you golden edges.

Duration: ten-twelve minutes

Nutrients (per portion, makes about forty-eight cookies):

- Caloric content: 90
- Fatty acid: three grams
- Carb content: fifteen grams
- Amino content: one gram

27. Peppermint Chocolate Cookies

Ingredients:

- one cupful (two bars) unsalted butter, softened

- one cupful granulated sugar
- three-fourth cupful brown sugar
- two large eggs
- two teaspoonful vanilla extract
- two one-fourth cupful all-purpose flour
- half cupful unsweetened cocoa powder
- one teaspoonful baking soda
- half teaspoonful salt
- one cupful semisweet chocolate chips
- one cupful crushed peppermint candies

Instructions:

1. Turn the oven temperature up to three hundred and seventy five degrees Fahrenheit (one hundred and eighty five degrees Celsius).

2. Cream the butter, white sugar, and brown sugar together in a large bowl.

3. Mix in the vanilla extract after each egg has been beaten in.

4. Separately, whisk together the dry ingredients (flour, cocoa powder, baking soda, and salt). Mix this up with the butter slowly.

5. Combine the chocolate chips and crushed peppermint candies by stirring them in.

6. Place dough by the spoonful on baking sheets that have not been oiled.

7. Cook for 8–ten minutes.

Duration: eight-ten minutes

Nutrients (per portion, makes about thirty-six cookies):

- Caloric content: one-fifty
- Fatty acid: six grams
- Carb content: twenty-four grams
- Amino content: two grams

28. Almond Snowball Cookies

Ingredients:

- one cupful (two bars) unsalted butter, softened
- half cupful powdered sugar
- one teaspoonful almond extract
- two one-fourth cupful all-purpose flour
- half teaspoonful salt
- three-fourth cupful finely chopped almonds
- Additional powdered sugar for rolling

Instructions:

1. The oven has to be Heat in advanceed to 400F (20C).

2. Butter and a half cupful of powdered sugar should be creamed together in a large bowl.

3. Blend with some almond extract.

4. Flour and salt should be mixed together in a separate basin. Mix this up with the butter slowly.

5. Add the almonds and mix well.

6. Roll the dough into one-inch balls and set them on baking pans that have not been oiled.

7. Put in the oven for ten–twelve minutes.

8. Roll the cookies in more powdered sugar while they're still hot.

9. Upon cooling, re-roll in powdered sugar.

Duration: ten-twelve minutes

Nutrients (per portion, makes about thirty-six cookies):

- Caloric content: Hundred
- Fatty acid: seven grams
- Carb content: eight grams
- Amino content: one gram

29. Pecan Sandies

Ingredients:

- one cupful (two bars) unsalted butter, softened
- half cupful powdered sugar
- two teaspoonful vanilla extract
- two cupful all-purpose flour
- one-fourth teaspoonful salt

- one cupful chopped pecans
- Additional powdered sugar for rolling

Instructions:

1. Get the oven up to temperature, preferably about 165F/75C.
2. Butter and a half cupful of powdered sugar should be creamed together in a large bowl.
3. Blend with some vanilla extract.
4. Flour and salt should be mixed together in a separate basin. Mix this up with the butter slowly.
5. Blend in some chopped pecans.
6. Roll the dough into one-inch balls and set them on baking pans that have not been oiled.
7. To get a light golden colour, bake for 15–7 minutes.
8. Roll the cookies in more powdered sugar while they're still hot.
9. Upon cooling, re-roll in powdered sugar.

Duration: fifteen-1seven minutes

Nutrients (per portion, makes about thirty-six cookies):

- Caloric content: one-twenty
- Fatty acid: nine grams
- Carb content: nine grams
- Amino content: one gram

30. Lemon Shortbread Cookies

Ingredients:

- one cupful (two bars) unsalted butter, softened
- half cupful powdered sugar
- one teaspoonful lemon zest
- two cupful all-purpose flour
- one-fourth teaspoonful salt
- one-fourth cupful lemon juice
- one cupful confectioners' sugar

Instructions:

1. Turn the oven temperature up to three hundred and seventy five degrees Fahrenheit (one hundred and eighty five degrees Celsius).

2. Combine the butter, confectioners' sugar, and lemon zest in a large bowl and beat until smooth.

3. Flour and salt should be mixed together in a separate basin. Mix this up with the butter slowly.

4. After the dough has rested in the fridge for thirty minutes, roll it into a log and cover it in plastic.

5. Rounds about one-fourth inch thick should be cut from the log and placed on baking pans coated with parchment paper.

6. Bake for 12–fifteen minutes, or until the edges are just beginning to turn brown.

7. Drizzle the lemon juice and confectioners' sugar mixture over the heated cookies.

Duration: twelve-fifteen minutes

Nutrients (per portion, makes about thirty-six cookies):

- Caloric content: one-ten
- Fatty acid: six grams
- Carb content: 1four grams
- Amino content: one gram

31. Snowball Cookies

Ingredients:

- one cupful (two bars) unsalted butter, softened
- half cupful powdered sugar
- one teaspoonful vanilla extract
- two one-fourth cupful all-purpose flour
- one-fourth teaspoonful salt
- three-fourth cupful finely chopped pecans
- Additional powdered sugar for rolling

Instructions:

1. Bake at 350 degrees Fahrenheit (one seventy-five degrees Celsius).

2. Combine the butter and half a cupful of the powdered sugar in a large bowl and beat until fluffy.

3. Add the vanilla essence and mix well.

4. Put the flour and salt in an other basin. Slowly incorporate this into the butter.

5. Add the pecan pieces and stir well.

6. The dough should be rolled into one-inch balls and then placed on baking pans that have not been buttered.

7. Bake for ten–twelve minutes.

8. The heated cookies need more powdered sugar, so roll them in it.

Duration: ten-twelve minutes

Nutrients (per portion, makes about thirty-six cookies):

- Caloric content: 90
- Fatty acid: six grams
- Carb content: eight grams
- Amino content: one gram

32. Cherry Almond Cookies

Ingredients:

- one cupful (two bars) unsalted butter, softened
- one cupful granulated sugar
- one large egg
- one teaspoonful almond extract

- two three-fourth cupful all-purpose flour
- half teaspoonful salt
- half cupful maraschino cherries, chopped
- half cupful slivered almonds

Instructions:

1. Turn the oven temperature up to three hundred and seventy five degrees Fahrenheit (one hundred and eighty five degrees Celsius).

2. Butter and granulated sugar should be creamed together in a large basin.

3. The egg and almond essence should be mixed in.

4. Flour and salt should be mixed separately. Mix this up with the butter slowly.

5. The almond slivers and chopped cherries should be combined.

6. Spoonful of cookie dough are dropped onto baking pans coated with paper.

7. Put in the oven for ten–twelve minutes.

Duration: ten-twelve minutes

Nutrients (per portion, makes about thirty-six cookies):

- Caloric content: one-twenty
- Fatty acid: seven grams
- Carb content: 1four grams
- Amino content: two grams

33. Chocolate Mint Cookies

Ingredients:

- one cupful (two bars) unsalted butter, softened
- one half cupful granulated sugar
- two large eggs
- one teaspoonful peppermint extract
- two cupful all-purpose flour
- half cupful unsweetened cocoa powder
- one teaspoonful baking soda
- half teaspoonful salt
- one cupful semisweet chocolate chips
- one cupful crushed peppermint candies

Instructions:

1. Turn the oven temperature up to three hundred and seventy five degrees Fahrenheit (one hundred and eighty five degrees Celsius).

2. Butter and granulated sugar should be creamed together in a large basin.

3. Peppermint essence and eggs should be mixed together.

4. Separately, whisk together the dry ingredients (flour, cocoa powder, baking soda, and salt). Mix this up with the butter slowly.

5. Combine the chocolate chips and crushed peppermint candies by stirring them in.

6. Spoonful of cookie dough are dropped onto baking pans coated with paper.

7. Cook for 8–ten minutes.

Duration: eight-ten minutes

Nutrients (per portion, makes about thirty-six cookies):

- Caloric content: one-fifty
- Fatty acid: seven grams
- Carb content: twenty-two grams
- Amino content: two grams

34. Cinnamon Sugar Cookies

Ingredients:

- one cupful (two bars) unsalted butter, softened
- one half cupful granulated sugar
- two large eggs
- one teaspoonful vanilla extract
- two three-fourth cupful all-purpose flour
- two teaspoonful cream of tartar
- one teaspoonful baking soda
- one-fourth teaspoonful salt
- two tablespoonful ground cinnamon
- two tablespoonful granulated sugar (for rolling)

Instructions:

1. Turn the oven temperature up to three hundred and seventy five degrees Fahrenheit (one hundred and eighty five degrees Celsius).

2. Butter and half a cupful of granulated sugar should be creamed together in a large bowl.

3. Add the egg and vanilla and mix well.

4. Flour, cream of tartar, baking soda, and salt should be combined in a separate basin and whisked together. Mix this up with the butter slowly.

5. Combine the ground cinnamon and the two tablespoonful of sugar in a separate small bowl and stir to combine.

6. Roll the dough into balls about an inch in diameter and coat with the cinnamon sugar.

7. You should bake the cookies on parchment paper.

8. Cook for 8–ten minutes.

Duration: eight-ten minutes

Nutrients (per portion, makes about thirty-six cookies):

- Caloric content: one-forty
- Fatty acid: six grams
- Carb content: twenty-one gram
- Amino content: two grams

35. Cranberry Pistachio Biscotti

Ingredients:

- half cupful (one bar) unsalted butter, softened
- three-fourth cupful granulated sugar

- two large eggs
- one teaspoonful almond extract
- two one-fourth cupful all-purpose flour
- one half teaspoonful baking powder
- half teaspoonful salt
- half cupful dried cranberries
- half cupful shelled pistachios

Instructions:

1. Turn the oven temperature up to three hundred and seventy five degrees Fahrenheit (one hundred and eighty five degrees Celsius).

2. Butter and granulated sugar should be creamed together in a large basin.

3. Cream the egg whites and almond extract together.

4. Flour, baking powder, and salt should be mixed together in a separate basin. Mix this up with the butter slowly.

5. Mix in the pistachios and dried cranberries.

6. Make two logs using the dough and place them on a baking pan coated with parchment paper.

7. Bake for 25–30 minutes, or until the logs are just beginning to turn brown.

8. After around ten minutes, cut the logs into biscotti.

9. Place the slices in a single layer on the baking sheet and bake for another ten–twelve minutes.

Duration: twenty five-thirty minutes (first bake) + ten-twelve minutes (second bake)

Nutrients (per portion, makes about twenty-four biscotti):

- Caloric content: one-fifty
- Fatty acid: seven grams
- Carb content: twenty grams
- Amino content: two grams

CHAPTER 8

SPECIALTY COOKIES

36. Raspberry Linzer Cookies

Ingredients:

- one cupful (two bars) unsalted butter, softened
- one cupful granulated sugar
- one large egg
- two teaspoonful vanilla extract
- two half cupful all-purpose flour
- one-fourth teaspoonful salt

- half cupful seedless raspberry jam
- Powdered sugar for dusting

Instructions:

1. Butter and granulated sugar should be creamed together in a large basin.

2. Add the egg and vanilla and mix well.

3. Flour and salt should be mixed separately. Mix this up with the butter slowly.

4. Form a disc using each half of the dough. Refrigerate for at least one hour after wrapping in plastic.

5. Turn the oven temperature up to three hundred and seventy five degrees Fahrenheit (one hundred and eighty five degrees Celsius).

6. On a floured surface, roll out one disc to a thickness of approximately half an inch.

7. Prepare an even number of cookies, with a little window cut out of the centre of half of them.

8. Put in the oven for ten–twelve minutes.

9. Please wait until the cookies cool.

10. Raspberry jam should be spread very thinly on the firm biscuits.

11. Sprinkle powdered sugar in between two of the window cookies and enjoy.

Duration: ten-twelve minutes

Nutrients (per portion, makes about twenty-four sandwich cookies):

- Caloric content: sixteen0

- Fatty acid: eight grams
- Carb content: twenty-one gram
- Amino content: one gram

37. Pistachio Cranberry Slice-and-Bake Cookies

Ingredients:

- one cupful (two bars) unsalted butter, softened
- one cupful granulated sugar
- one large egg
- one teaspoonful vanilla extract
- two half cupful all-purpose flour
- half teaspoonful salt
- half cupful chopped pistachios
- half cupful dried cranberries

Instructions:

1. Butter and granulated sugar should be creamed together in a large basin.
2. Add the egg and vanilla and mix well.
3. Flour and salt should be mixed together in a separate basin. Mix this up with the butter slowly.
4. Add the pistachios and cranberries and mix well.
5. Form two equal-sized logs from the dough.
6. Refrigerate for at least one hour after wrapping in plastic.

7. Turn the oven temperature up to three hundred and seventy five degrees Fahrenheit (one hundred and eighty five degrees Celsius).

8. Cut the logs into 1/4-inch thick circles and arrange on baking pans lined with parchment paper.

9. Put in the oven for ten–twelve minutes.

Duration: ten-twelve minutes

Nutrients (per portion, makes about thirty-six cookies):

- Caloric content: one-twenty
- Fatty acid: six grams
- Carb content: fifteen grams
- Amino content: one gram

38. Lemon Meltaways

Ingredients:

- one cupful (two bars) unsalted butter, softened
- half cupful powdered sugar
- one teaspoonful lemon zest
- two tablespoonful fresh lemon juice
- two cupful all-purpose flour
- one-fourth teaspoonful salt
- Additional powdered sugar for rolling

Instructions:

1. Butter and a half cupful of powdered sugar should be creamed together in a large bowl.

2. Add the lemon juice and zest and mix well.

3. Flour and salt should be mixed separately. Mix this up with the butter slowly.

4. Form the dough into a log, cover it in plastic, and refrigerate it for at least an hour.

5. Turn the oven temperature up to three hundred and seventy five degrees Fahrenheit (one hundred and eighty five degrees Celsius).

6. Cut the log into 1/4-inch thick circles, then arrange on baking pans lined with parchment paper.

7. Put in the oven for ten–twelve minutes.

8. While still hot, roll the cookies in more powdered sugar.

Duration: ten-twelve minutes

Nutrients (per portion, makes about thirty-six cookies):

- Caloric content: 90
- Fatty acid: six grams
- Carb content: eight grams
- Amino content: one gram

39. Cherry Almond Biscotti

Ingredients:

- half cupful (one bar) unsalted butter, softened

- one cupful granulated sugar
- two large eggs
- one teaspoonful almond extract
- two half cupful all-purpose flour
- half teaspoonful baking powder
- one-fourth teaspoonful salt
- half cupful dried cherries
- half cupful slivered almonds

Instructions:

1. Turn the oven temperature up to three hundred and seventy five degrees Fahrenheit (one hundred and eighty five degrees Celsius).

2. Butter and granulated sugar should be creamed together in a large basin.

3. Cream the egg whites and almond extract together.

4. Flour, baking powder, and salt should be mixed together in a separate basin. Mix this up with the butter slowly.

5. Add the dried fruit and almonds and mix well.

6. Make two logs using the dough and place them on a baking pan coated with parchment paper.

7. Bake for 25–30 minutes, or until the logs are just beginning to turn brown.

8. After around ten minutes, cut the logs into biscotti.

Duration: twenty five-thirty minutes (first bake) + Additional time for cooling and slicing

Nutrients (per portion, makes about twenty-four biscotti):

- Caloric content: one-thirty
- Fatty acid: seven grams
- Carb content: fifteen grams
- Amino content: two grams

40. Pomegranate White Chocolate Cookies

Ingredients:

- one cupful (two bars) unsalted butter, softened
- one cupful granulated sugar
- two large eggs
- one teaspoonful vanilla extract
- two half cupful all-purpose flour
- half teaspoonful baking soda
- half teaspoonful salt
- half cupful pomegranate seeds
- one cupful white chocolate chips

Instructions:

1. Turn the oven temperature up to three hundred and seventy five degrees Fahrenheit (one hundred and eighty five degrees Celsius).

2. Butter and granulated sugar should be creamed together in a large basin.

3. Add the egg and vanilla and mix well.

4. Separately, combine the flour, baking powder, and salt in a bowl and mix. Mix this up with the butter slowly.

5. Mix in the white chocolate chips and pomegranate seeds.

6. Spoonful of cookie dough are dropped onto baking pans coated with paper.

7. Put in the oven for ten–twelve minutes.

Duration: ten-twelve minutes

Nutrients (per portion, makes about thirty-six cookies):

- Caloric content: one-thirty
- Fatty acid: seven grams
- Carb content: sixteen grams
- Amino content: one gram

41. Mocha Swirl Cookies

Ingredients:

- half cupful (one bar) unsalted butter, softened
- half cupful granulated sugar
- one large egg
- one teaspoonful vanilla extract
- one three-fourth cupful all-purpose flour
- one-fourth cupful unsweetened cocoa powder

- one teaspoonful instant coffee granules
- half teaspoonful baking powder
- one-fourth teaspoonful salt
- half cupful semisweet chocolate chips
- half cupful white chocolate chips

Instructions:

1. Turn the oven temperature up to three hundred and seventy five degrees Fahrenheit (one hundred and eighty five degrees Celsius).

2. Butter and granulated sugar should be creamed together in a large basin.

3. Add the egg and vanilla and mix well.

4. Flour, cocoa powder, instant coffee granules, baking powder, and salt should be mixed together in a separate basin. Mix this up with the butter slowly.

5. Cut the dough in two equal pieces.

6. The semisweet chocolate chips go in one bowl.

7. Incorporate the white chocolate chips into the other half.

8. Marble your dough by taking a tiny amount of each colour and twisting it together.

9. Spoonful of the marbled dough should be dropped onto baking pans coated with parchment paper.

10. Put in the oven for ten–twelve minutes.

Duration: ten-twelve minutes

Nutrients (per portion, makes about thirty-six cookies):

- Caloric content: Hundred
- Fatty acid: five grams
- Carb content: 1four grams
- Amino content: one gram

42. Cinnamon Roll Cookies

Ingredients:

- one cupful (two bars) unsalted butter, softened
- one cupful granulated sugar
- two large eggs
- one teaspoonful vanilla extract
- two half cupful all-purpose flour
- half teaspoonful salt
- one teaspoonful ground cinnamon
- one-fourth cupful finely chopped pecans
- one-fourth cupful raisins

Instructions:

1. Butter and granulated sugar should be creamed together in a large basin.

2. Add the egg and vanilla and mix well.

3. Flour, salt, and ground cinnamon should be mixed together in a separate basin. Mix this up with the butter slowly.

4. Mix in the raisins and finely chopped pecans.

5. Cut the dough in two equal pieces.

6. Turn each section into a log.

7. Put the two logs together and turn them into one.

8. Prepare baking pans lined with parchment paper and cut the twisted log into 1/4-inch thick circles.

9. Put in the oven for ten–twelve minutes.

Duration: ten-twelve minutes

Nutrients (per portion, makes about thirty-six cookies):

- Caloric content: one-twenty

- Fatty acid: six grams

- Carb content: fifteen grams

- Amino content: one gram

43. Tiramisu Cookies

Ingredients:

- one cupful (two bars) unsalted butter, softened

- one cupful granulated sugar

- two large eggs

- one teaspoonful instant espresso powder

- one teaspoonful vanilla extract

- two half cupful all-purpose flour

- half teaspoonful baking powder
- one-fourth teaspoonful salt
- one-fourth cupful mascarpone cheese
- one-fourth cupful brewed espresso, cooled
- one-fourth cupful unsweetened cocoa powder

Instructions:

1. Turn the oven temperature up to three hundred and seventy five degrees Fahrenheit (one hundred and eighty five degrees Celsius).

2. Butter and granulated sugar should be creamed together in a large basin.

3. Mix in the eggs, espresso powder, and vanilla.

4. Flour, baking powder, and salt should be mixed together in a separate basin. Mix this up with the butter slowly.

5. Spoonful of cookie dough are dropped onto baking pans coated with paper.

6. Put in the oven for ten–twelve minutes.

7. Please wait until the cookies cool.

8. Mascarpone cheese, brewed espresso, and unsweetened cocoa powder should be mixed in a small bowl.

9. One cookie should have the espresso filling spread on the bottom, and another cookie should be used as a sandwich.

Duration: ten-twelve minutes

Nutrients (per portion, makes about thirty-six cookies):

- Caloric content: one-ten
- Fatty acid: six grams
- Carb content: thirteen grams
- Amino content: one gram

44. Chocolate Hazelnut Thumbprint Cookies

Ingredients:

- half cupful (one bar) unsalted butter, softened
- half cupful granulated sugar
- one large egg
- one teaspoonful vanilla extract
- one three-fourth cupful all-purpose flour
- half cupful unsweetened cocoa powder
- half teaspoonful salt
- half cupful chopped hazelnuts
- Nutella or chocolate hazelnut spread for filling

Instructions:

1. Turn the oven temperature up to three hundred and seventy five degrees Fahrenheit (one hundred and eighty five degrees Celsius).

2. Butter and granulated sugar should be creamed together in a large basin.

3. Add the egg and vanilla and mix well.

4. Flour, cocoa powder, and salt should be mixed together in a separate basin. Mix this up with the butter slowly.

5. Roll the dough into one-inch balls and arrange them on baking pans lined with parchment paper.

6. Put your thumb in the middle of each cookie to make a depression.

7. Put in the oven for ten–twelve minutes.

8. Please wait until the cookies cool.

9. Spread Nutella or another chocolate hazelnut spread into the craters.

Duration: ten-twelve minutes

Nutrients (per portion, makes about thirty-six cookies):

- Caloric content: one-ten
- Fatty acid: six grams
- Carb content: 1four grams
- Amino content: one gram

45. Orange Cardamom Sable Cookies

Ingredients:

- one cupful (two bars) unsalted butter, softened
- half cupful granulated sugar
- one large egg
- two teaspoonful orange zest
- two half cupful all-purpose flour

- half teaspoonful ground cardamom
- one-fourth teaspoonful salt
- one-fourth cupful sanding sugar (for decoration)

Instructions:

1. Butter and granulated sugar should be creamed together in a large basin.

2. Add the egg and orange zest and mix well.

3. Flour, ground cardamom, and salt should be mixed together in a separate basin. Mix this up with the butter slowly.

4. Form the dough into a log, cover it in plastic, and refrigerate it for at least an hour.

5. Turn the oven temperature up to three hundred and seventy five degrees Fahrenheit (one hundred and eighty five degrees Celsius).

6. Cut the log into 1/4-inch thick circles, then arrange on baking pans lined with parchment paper.

7. Each cookie should be dusted with sanding sugar.

8. Put in the oven for ten–twelve minutes.

Duration: ten-twelve minutes

Nutrients (per portion, makes about thirty-six cookies):

- Caloric content: Hundred
- Fatty acid: six grams
- Carb content: 1one gram

- Amino content: one gram

46. Caramel Apple Thumbprint Cookies

Ingredients:

- one cupful (two bars) unsalted butter, softened
- one cupful granulated sugar
- two large eggs
- one teaspoonful vanilla extract
- two half cupful all-purpose flour
- half teaspoonful salt
- half cupful finely chopped dried apples
- one-fourth cupful caramel sauce

Instructions:

1. Turn the oven temperature up to three hundred and seventy five degrees Fahrenheit (one hundred and eighty five degrees Celsius).

2. Butter and granulated sugar should be creamed together in a large basin.

3. Add the egg and vanilla and mix well.

4. Flour and salt should be mixed separately. Mix this up with the butter slowly.

5. Roll the dough into one-inch balls and arrange them on baking pans lined with parchment paper.

6. Put your thumb in the middle of each cookie to make a depression.

7. Put in the oven for ten–twelve minutes.

8. Please wait until the cookies cool.

9. Spread caramel sauce in the hollows.

Duration: ten-twelve minutes

Nutrients (per portion, makes about thirty-six cookies):

- Caloric content: one-twenty

- Fatty acid: six grams

- Carb content: fifteen grams

- Amino content: one gram

47. Peppermint Bark Cookies

Ingredients:

- one cupful (two bars) unsalted butter, softened

- one cupful granulated sugar

- one large egg

- one teaspoonful peppermint extract

- two half cupful all-purpose flour

- half cupful unsweetened cocoa powder

- half teaspoonful salt

- half cupful crushed candy canes

- half cupful semisweet chocolate chips

Instructions:

1. Turn the oven temperature up to three hundred and seventy five degrees Fahrenheit (one hundred and eighty five degrees Celsius).

2. Butter and granulated sugar should be creamed together in a large basin.

3. Cream the egg and peppermint essence together.

4. Flour, cocoa powder, and salt should be mixed together in a separate basin. Mix this up with the butter slowly.

5. Combine the chocolate chips and crushed candy canes.

6. Spoonful of cookie dough are dropped onto baking pans coated with paper.

7. Put in the oven for ten–twelve minutes.

Duration: ten-twelve minutes

Nutrients (per portion, makes about thirty-six cookies):

- Caloric content: one-twenty
- Fatty acid: six grams
- Carb content: fifteen grams
- Amino content: one gram

48. Eggnog Snickerdoodles

Ingredients:

- one cupful (two bars) unsalted butter, softened
- one half cupful granulated sugar
- two large eggs

- one teaspoonful vanilla extract
- half cupful eggnog
- four cupful all-purpose flour
- half teaspoonful salt
- half teaspoonful ground nutmeg
- half teaspoonful ground cinnamon
- one-fourth teaspoonful cream of tartar
- two tablespoonful granulated sugar
- one teaspoonful ground nutmeg

Instructions:

1. It is recommended that the oven be Heat in advanceed at three hundred and seventy five degrees Fahrenheit (190 degrees Celsius).

2. Butter and half a cupful of granulated sugar should be creamed together in a large bowl.

3. Eggs, vanilla, and eggnog should be mixed together.

4. Flour, salt, nutmeg, cinnamon, and cream of tartar should be mixed together in a separate basin. Mix this into the eggnog slowly.

5. Two tablespoonful of sugar and a teaspoonful of nutmeg should be mixed together in a separate basin.

6. Roll one-inch balls of dough in the sugar-nutmeg mixture to coat.

7. You should bake the cookies on parchment paper.

8. Cook for 8–ten minutes.

Duration: eight-ten minutes

Nutrients (per portion, makes about forty-eight cookies):

- Caloric content: 90
- Fatty acid: four grams
- Carb content: twelve grams
- Amino content: one gram

49. Chocolate-Dipped Almond Biscotti

Ingredients:

- half cupful (one bar) unsalted butter, softened
- one cupful granulated sugar
- two large eggs
- one teaspoonful almond extract
- two half cupful all-purpose flour
- one half teaspoonful baking powder
- one-fourth teaspoonful salt
- half cupful slivered almonds
- six oz semisweet chocolate, melted

Instructions:

1. Turn the oven temperature up to three hundred and seventy five degrees Fahrenheit (one hundred and eighty five degrees Celsius).

2. Butter and granulated sugar should be creamed together in a large basin.

3. Cream the egg whites and almond extract together.

4. Flour, baking powder, and salt should be mixed together in a separate basin. Mix this up with the butter slowly.

5. Add the sliced almonds and mix well.

6. Make two logs using the dough and place them on a baking pan coated with parchment paper.

7. Bake for 25–30 minutes, or until the logs are just beginning to turn brown.

8. After around ten minutes, cut the logs into biscotti.

9. Put melted semisweet chocolate on one end of each biscotti.

Duration: twenty five-thirty minutes (first bake) + Additional time for cooling and dipping

Nutrients (per portion, makes about twenty-four biscotti):

- Caloric content: one-fifty
- Fatty acid: seven grams
- Carb content: twenty grams
- Amino content: two grams

50. Maple Pecan Pie Cookies

Ingredients:

- one cupful (two bars) unsalted butter, softened
- one cupful packed brown sugar

- one large egg
- one teaspoonful vanilla extract
- half cupful pure maple syrup
- two half cupful all-purpose flour
- half teaspoonful baking soda
- one-fourth teaspoonful salt
- one cupful chopped pecans

Instructions:

1. Turn the oven temperature up to three hundred and seventy five degrees Fahrenheit (one hundred and eighty five degrees Celsius).

2. Butter and brown sugar should be creamed together in a large bowl.

3. Combine the egg, vanilla, and maple syrup and beat until smooth.

4. Flour, baking powder, and salt should be mixed together in a separate basin. Mix this up with the butter slowly.

5. Blend in some chopped pecans.

6. Spoonful of cookie dough are dropped onto baking pans coated with paper.

7. Put in the oven for ten–twelve minutes.

Duration: ten-twelve minutes

Nutrients (per portion, makes about thirty-six cookies):

- Caloric content: one-thirty
- Fatty acid: seven grams

- Carb content: sixteen grams
- Amino content: two grams

51. Cranberry Pistachio White Chocolate Chip Cookies

Ingredients:

- one cupful (two bars) unsalted butter, softened
- one cupful granulated sugar
- two large eggs
- one teaspoonful vanilla extract
- two half cupful all-purpose flour
- half teaspoonful baking soda
- half teaspoonful salt
- one cupful dried cranberries
- half cupful shelled pistachios
- one cupful white chocolate chips

Instructions:

1. Turn the oven temperature up to three hundred and seventy five degrees Fahrenheit (one hundred and eighty five degrees Celsius).

2. Butter and granulated sugar should be creamed together in a large basin.

3. Add the egg and vanilla and mix well.

4. Separately, combine the flour, baking powder, and salt in a bowl and mix. Mix this up with the butter slowly.

5. Mix in some pistachios, white chocolate chips, and dried cranberries.

6. Spoonful of cookie dough are dropped onto baking pans coated with paper.

7. Put in the oven for ten–twelve minutes.

Duration: ten-twelve minutes

Nutrients (per portion, makes about thirty-six cookies):

- Caloric content: one-forty
- Fatty acid: seven grams
- Carb content: eighteen grams
- Amino content: two grams

52. Chocolate Peppermint Sandwich Cookies

Ingredients:

- one cupful (two bars) unsalted butter, softened
- one cupful granulated sugar
- two large eggs
- one teaspoonful vanilla extract
- two cupful all-purpose flour
- half cupful unsweetened cocoa powder
- half teaspoonful salt
- half teaspoonful baking powder
- half teaspoonful baking soda

- half cupful crushed candy canes
- one cupful semisweet chocolate chips
- half cupful heavy cream
- half teaspoonful peppermint extract

Instructions: *For the Cookies:*

1. Turn the oven temperature up to three hundred and seventy five degrees Fahrenheit (one hundred and eighty five degrees Celsius).

2. Butter and granulated sugar should be creamed together in a large basin.

3. Add the egg and vanilla and mix well.

4. Flour, cocoa powder, salt, baking soda, and baking powder should be mixed together in a separate basin. Mix this up with the butter slowly.

5. Candy canes, crushed, should be added.

6. Spoonful of cookie dough are dropped onto baking pans coated with paper.

7. Cook for 8–ten minutes.

For the Filling:

1. Heavy cream should be heated until it is almost boiling in a small pot.

2. In a heat-safe dish, combine the chocolate chips and hot cream and let settle for one minute.

3. Chocolate should be stirred until it is totally melted and smooth.

4. Peppermint extract should be mixed in now.

5. Please wait as the chocolate filling thickens and cools.

Assembly:

1. On the bottom of one cookie, spread a lot of the chocolate-peppermint filling.

2. Put another biscuit in between.

3. Let the filling cool and harden.

Cook Time (for cookies): eight-ten minutes

Nutrients (per portion, makes about twenty-four sandwich cookies):

- Caloric content: twenty five0

- Fatty acid: fifteen grams

- Carb content: 2eight grams

- Amino content: three grams

53. Orange Cranberry Shortbread Cookies

Ingredients:

- one cupful (two bars) unsalted butter, softened

- half cupful powdered sugar

- one teaspoonful orange zest

- two half cupful all-purpose flour

- half teaspoonful salt

- half cupful dried cranberries

- one-fourth cupful fresh orange juice

- Additional powdered sugar for rolling

Instructions:

1. Cream the butter and confectioners' sugar together in a large bowl.

2. Add the orange zest and stir.

3. Flour and salt should be mixed separately. Mix this up with the butter slowly.

4. Blend together some fresh orange juice and dried cranberries.

5. Form the dough into a log, cover it with plastic wrap, and refrigerate it for at least an hour.

6. Get the oven up to temperature, preferably about 165F/75C.

7. Rounds about one-fourth inch thick should be cut from the log and placed on baking pans coated with parchment paper.

8. Dust more powdered sugar on the outside edges.

9. Put it in the oven for twelve-fifteen minutes.

Duration: twelve-fifteen minutes

Nutrients (per portion, makes about thirty-six cookies):

- Caloric content: 90
- Fatty acid: six grams
- Carb content: ten grams
- Amino content: one gram

54. Mint Chocolate Crinkle Cookies

Ingredients:

- half cupful (one bar) unsalted butter, softened

- one cupful granulated sugar
- two large eggs
- one teaspoonful peppermint extract
- one three-fourth cupful all-purpose flour
- half cupful unsweetened cocoa powder
- one half teaspoonful baking powder
- one-fourth teaspoonful salt
- half cupful semisweet chocolate chips
- Powdered sugar for rolling

Instructions:

1. Turn the oven temperature up to three hundred and seventy five degrees Fahrenheit (one hundred and eighty five degrees Celsius).

2. Butter and granulated sugar should be creamed together in a large basin.

3. Peppermint essence and eggs should be mixed together.

4. Flour, cocoa powder, baking soda, and salt should be mixed together in a separate basin. Mix this up with the butter slowly.

5. Combine in the semisweet chocolate chips.

6. Form the dough into balls, about one inch in diameter, and coat them in powdered sugar.

7. You should bake the cookies on parchment paper.

8. Put in the oven for ten–twelve minutes.

Duration: ten-twelve minutes

Nutrients (per portion, makes about thirty-six cookies):

- Caloric content: Hundred
- Fatty acid: four grams
- Carb content: fifteen grams
- Amino content: one gram

55. Chocolate Caramel Thumbprint Cookies

Ingredients:

- one cupful (two bars) unsalted butter, softened
- one cupful granulated sugar
- one large egg
- one teaspoonful vanilla extract
- two one-fourth cupful all-purpose flour
- half cupful unsweetened cocoa powder
- one-fourth teaspoonful salt
- one cupful caramel-filled chocolate candies
- one-fourth cupful semisweet chocolate chips

Instructions:

1. Turn the oven temperature up to three hundred and seventy five degrees Fahrenheit (one hundred and eighty five degrees Celsius).

2. Butter and granulated sugar should be creamed together in a large basin.

3. Add the egg and vanilla and mix well.

4. Flour, cocoa powder, and salt should be mixed together in a separate basin. Mix this up with the butter slowly.

5. Roll the dough into one-inch balls and arrange them on baking pans lined with parchment paper.

6. Put your thumb in the middle of each cookie to make a depression.

7. Put in the oven for ten–twelve minutes.

8. Put a chocolate candy filled with caramel in the middle of each hot biscuit.

9. Let the chocolate melt a little bit.

10. Melt some semisweet chocolate and drizzle it over top.

Duration: ten-twelve minutes

Nutrients (per portion, makes about thirty-six cookies):

- Caloric content: one-twenty

- Fatty acid: six grams

- Carb content: sixteen grams

- Amino content: one gram

CHAPTER 9

HEALTHY AND GLUTEN-FREE OPTIONS

56. Almond Flour Chocolate Chip Cookies

Ingredients:

- two cupful almond flour
- half teaspoonful baking soda
- one-fourth teaspoonful salt
- one-fourth cupful coconut oil, melted
- one-fourth cupful pure maple syrup
- one large egg

- one teaspoonful pure vanilla extract
- half cupful dark chocolate chips

Instructions:

1. Heat in advance your oven to 350°F, One hundred and Seventy Five degrees Celsius

2. In a mixing bowl, combine the almond flour, baking soda, and salt.

3. In another bowl, whisk together the melted coconut oil, maple syrup, egg, and vanilla extract.

4. Combine the wet and dry ingredients and fold in the chocolate chips.

5. Drop rounded tablespoonful of dough onto a baking sheet lined with parchment paper.

6. Flatten each cookie slightly.

7. Bake for ten-twelve minutes or until the edges are golden.

8. Allow cookies to cool on the baking sheet for a few minutes before transferring them to a wire rack to cool completely.

Duration: twelve minutes

Nutrients (per portion):

- Caloric content: 140
- Fatty acid: 11g
- Carb content: 9g
- Amino content: 3g

57. Coconut Macaroons

Ingredients:

- two two-third cupful shredded coconut
- half cupful sweetened condensed milk (use a gluten-free brand)
- two large egg whites
- one teaspoonful pure vanilla extract
- one-fourth teaspoonful salt
- four oz dark chocolate, melted (for drizzling)

Instructions:

1. Heat in advance your oven to 325°F (160°C).

2. In a mixing bowl, combine the shredded coconut, sweetened condensed milk, egg whites, vanilla extract, and salt.

3. Drop rounded tablespoonful of the mixture onto a baking sheet lined with parchment paper.

4. Bake for 15-eighteen minutes or until the macaroons are golden on the outside.

5. Allow the macaroons to cool on the baking sheet for a few minutes before transferring them to a wire rack.

6. Drizzle melted dark chocolate over the cooled macaroons.

Duration: eighteen minutes

Nutrients (per portion):

- Caloric content: 120

- Fatty acid: 7g
- Carb content: 14g
- Amino content: 2g

58. Gluten-Free Oatmeal Cookies

Ingredients:

- two half cupful gluten-free rolled oats
- one cupful almond flour
- half teaspoonful baking soda
- half teaspoonful ground cinnamon
- one-fourth teaspoonful salt
- half cupful coconut oil, melted
- half cupful pure maple syrup
- one large egg
- one teaspoonful pure vanilla extract
- half cupful raisins or dark chocolate chips

Instructions:

1. Heat in advance your oven to 350°F, One hundred and Seventy Five degrees Celsius

2. In a mixing bowl, combine the rolled oats, almond flour, baking soda, cinnamon, and salt.

3. In another bowl, whisk together the melted coconut oil, maple syrup, egg, and vanilla extract.

4. Combine the wet and dry ingredients, then fold in the raisins or dark chocolate chips.

5. Drop rounded tablespoonful of dough onto a baking sheet lined with parchment paper.

6. Flatten each cookie slightly.

7. Bake for twelve-fifteen minutes or until the edges are golden.

8. Allow cookies to cool on the baking sheet for a few minutes before transferring them to a wire rack to cool completely.

Duration: fifteen minutes

Nutrients (per portion):

- Caloric content: 140
- Fatty acid: 8g
- Carb content: 16g
- Amino content: 2g

59. Quinoa Chocolate Cookies

Ingredients:

- one cupful cooked quinoa, cooled
- half cupful almond butter
- one-fourth cupful unsweetened cocoa powder

- one-fourth cupful pure maple syrup
- one large egg
- one teaspoonful pure vanilla extract
- one-fourth teaspoonful baking powder
- one-fourth cupful dark chocolate chips

Instructions:

1. Heat in advance your oven to 350°F, One hundred and Seventy Five degrees Celsius

2. In a food processor, blend the cooked quinoa, almond butter, cocoa powder, maple syrup, egg, vanilla extract, and baking powder until smooth.

3. Stir in the dark chocolate chips.

4. Drop rounded tablespoonful of the mixture onto a baking sheet lined with parchment paper.

5. Bake for ten-twelve minutes or until the cookies are set.

6. Allow cookies to cool on the baking sheet for a few minutes before transferring them to a wire rack to cool completely.

Duration: twelve minutes

Nutrients (per portion):

- Caloric content: 120
- Fatty acid: 7g
- Carb content: 13g

- Amino content: 4g

60. Gluten-Free Peanut Butter Cookies

Ingredients:

- one cupful natural peanut butter
- half cupful pure maple syrup
- one large egg
- one teaspoonful pure vanilla extract

Instructions:

1. Heat in advance your oven to 350°F, One hundred and Seventy Five degrees Celsius

2. In a mixing bowl, combine the peanut butter, maple syrup, egg, and vanilla extract.

3. Drop rounded tablespoonful of the mixture onto a baking sheet lined with parchment paper.

4. Flatten each cookie slightly with a fork, creating a crisscross pattern.

5. Bake for ten-twelve minutes or until the edges are golden.

6. Allow cookies to cool on the baking sheet for a few minutes before transferring them to a wire rack to cool completely.

Duration: twelve minutes

Nutrients (per portion):

- Caloric content: 120

- Fatty acid: 8g

- Carb content: ten grams

- Amino content: 4g

61. Gluten-Free Banana Cookies

Ingredients:

- two ripe bananas, mashed

- half cupful almond butter

- one-fourth cupful pure maple syrup

- one large egg

- one teaspoonful pure vanilla extract

- one half cupful gluten-free rolled oats

- half teaspoonful baking soda

- half teaspoonful ground cinnamon

- one-fourth teaspoonful salt

- one-fourth cupful dark chocolate chips

Instructions:

1. Heat in advance your oven to 350°F, One hundred and Seventy Five degrees Celsius

2. In a mixing bowl, combine the mashed bananas, almond butter, maple syrup, egg, and vanilla extract.

3. In another bowl, mix together the rolled oats, baking soda, cinnamon, and salt.

4. Combine the wet and dry ingredients, then fold in the dark chocolate chips.

5. Drop rounded tablespoonful of dough onto a baking sheet lined with parchment paper.

6. Flatten each cookie slightly.

7. Bake for ten-twelve minutes or until the edges are golden.

8. Allow cookies to cool on the baking sheet for a few minutes before transferring them to a wire rack to cool completely.

Duration: twelve minutes

Nutrients (per portion):

- Caloric content: 130
- Fatty acid: 7g
- Carb content: 15g
- Amino content: 3g

62. Gluten-Free Coconut Flour Sugar Cookies

Ingredients:

- half cupful coconut flour
- one-fourth cupful coconut oil, melted
- one-fourth cupful pure maple syrup
- one large egg
- one teaspoonful pure vanilla extract

For Icing:

- half cupful confectioners' sugar
- one-two tablespoonful coconut milk
- Food coloring (optional)

Instructions:

1. Heat in advance your oven to 350°F, One hundred and Seventy Five degrees Celsius

2. In a mixing bowl, combine the coconut flour, melted coconut oil, maple syrup, egg, and vanilla extract.

3. The dough may be crumbly, but press it together and form it into a disk.

4. Roll out the dough on a surface dusted with coconut flour to about 1/4-inch thickness.

5. Cut out cookies using your favorite cookie cutters.

6. Place cookies on a baking sheet lined with parchment paper.

7. Bake for ten-twelve minutes or until the edges are golden.

8. Allow cookies to cool on the baking sheet for a few minutes before transferring them to a wire rack to cool completely.

9. For the icing, whisk together confectioners' sugar and coconut milk until you reach the desired consistency. Add food coloring if desired.

10. Decorate the cooled cookies with the icing.

Duration: twelve minutes

Nutrients (per portion):

- Caloric content: 70
- Fatty acid: 4g
- Carb content: 9g
- Amino content: 1g

63. Gluten-Free Zucchini Chocolate Chip Cookies

Ingredients:

- one cupful grated zucchini (excess moisture squeezed out)
- one-fourth cupful coconut oil, melted
- one-fourth cupful pure maple syrup
- one large egg
- one teaspoonful pure vanilla extract
- one one-fourth cupful almond flour
- one-fourth cupful unsweetened cocoa powder
- half teaspoonful baking soda
- one-fourth teaspoonful salt
- half cupful dark chocolate chips

Instructions:

1. Heat in advance your oven to 350°F, One hundred and Seventy Five degrees Celsius

2. In a mixing bowl, combine the grated zucchini, melted coconut oil, maple syrup, egg, and vanilla extract.

3. In another bowl, mix together the almond flour, cocoa powder, baking soda, and salt.

4. Combine the wet and dry ingredients and fold in the dark chocolate chips.

5. Drop rounded tablespoonful of dough onto a baking sheet lined with parchment paper.

6. Flatten each cookie slightly.

7. Bake for twelve-fifteen minutes or until the edges are set.

8. Allow cookies to cool on the baking sheet for a few minutes before transferring them to a wire rack to cool completely.

Duration: fifteen minutes

Nutrients (per portion):

- Caloric content: 120
- Fatty acid: 8g
- Carb content: 12g
- Amino content: 3g

64. Gluten-Free Chickpea Chocolate Cookies

Ingredients:

- one can (fifteen oz) chickpeas, drained and rinsed
- half cupful almond butter

- one-fourth cupful pure maple syrup
- one large egg
- one teaspoonful pure vanilla extract
- one-fourth cupful unsweetened cocoa powder
- half teaspoonful baking powder
- one-fourth teaspoonful salt
- one-fourth cupful dark chocolate chips

Instructions:

1. Heat in advance your oven to 350°F, One hundred and Seventy Five degrees Celsius

2. In a food processor, combine the chickpeas, almond butter, maple syrup, egg, and vanilla extract until smooth.

3. Add the cocoa powder, baking powder, and salt, and blend again until well combined.

4. Stir in the dark chocolate chips.

5. Drop rounded tablespoonful of the mixture onto a baking sheet lined with parchment paper.

6. Flatten each cookie slightly.

7. Bake for ten-twelve minutes or until the cookies are set.

8. Allow cookies to cool on the baking sheet for a few minutes before transferring them to a wire rack to cool completely.

Duration: twelve minutes

Nutrients (per portion):

- Caloric content: one hundred ten
- Fatty acid: 6g
- Carb content: 13g
- Amino content: 3g

65. Gluten-Free Banana Oatmeal Breakfast Cookies

Ingredients:

- two ripe bananas, mashed
- half cupful almond butter
- one-fourth cupful pure maple syrup
- one large egg
- one teaspoonful pure vanilla extract
- two cupful gluten-free rolled oats
- half teaspoonful ground cinnamon
- one-fourth teaspoonful salt
- one-fourth cupful dark chocolate chips
- one-fourth cupful chopped nuts (optional)

Instructions:

1. Heat in advance your oven to 350°F, One hundred and Seventy Five degrees Celsius

2. In a mixing bowl, combine the mashed bananas, almond butter, maple syrup, egg, and vanilla extract.

3. Add the gluten-free rolled oats, ground cinnamon, salt, dark chocolate chips, and nuts if desired.

4. Drop rounded tablespoonful of the mixture onto a baking sheet lined with parchment paper.

5. Flatten each cookie slightly.

6. Bake for twelve-fifteen minutes or until the edges are golden.

7. Allow cookies to cool on the baking sheet for a few minutes before transferring them to a wire rack to cool completely.

Duration: fifteen minutes

Nutrients (per portion):

- Caloric content: 130
- Fatty acid: 7g
- Carb content: 16g
- Amino content: 3g

66. Sparkling Cookies

Ingredients:

- one cupful (two bars) unsalted butter, softened
- one cupful granulated sugar
- one large egg

- one teaspoonful vanilla extract
- two half cupful all-purpose flour
- half teaspoonful salt
- Silver or white sanding sugar
- Royal icing for decorating

Instructions:

1. Butter and sugar should be creamed together in a large basin.
2. Add the egg and vanilla and mix well.
3. Flour and salt should be mixed separately. Mix this up with the butter slowly.
4. Use a rolling pin to form the dough into snowflakes.
5. You should bake the cookies on parchment paper.
6. The cookies would look great dusted with silver or white sanding sugar.
7. Cook for 8–10 minutes.
8. Royal icing is best for decorating cookies after they have cooled.

Duration: eight-ten minutes

Nutrients (per serving, makes about thirty-six cookies):

- Caloric content: one-thirty
- Fatty acid: six grams
- Carb content: eighteen grams
- Amino content: one gram

67. Vanilla Cookies

Ingredients:

- one cupful (two bars) unsalted butter, softened
- one cupful granulated sugar
- one large egg
- one teaspoonful vanilla extract
- two half cupful all-purpose flour
- half teaspoonful salt
- Mini pretzels (antlers)
- Red M&M candies (noses)
- Royal icing for decorating
- Mini chocolate chips or brown icing (eyes)

Instructions:

1. Butter and sugar should be creamed together in a large basin.
2. Add the egg and vanilla and mix well.
3. Flour and salt should be mixed separately. Mix this up with the butter slowly.
4. Cut out reindeer forms from the dough after rolling it out.
5. You should bake the cookies on parchment paper.
6. For the antlers, use small pretzels; for the nose, use red M&Ms; and for the eyes, use either micro chocolate chips or brown icing.

7. Cook for 8–10 minutes.
8. Once the cookies have cooled, use royal icing to add any finishing touches you'd like.

Duration: eight-ten minutes

Nutrients (per serving, makes about thirty-six cookies):

- Caloric content: one-forty
- Fatty acid: six grams
- Carb content: twenty grams
- Amino content: one gram

68. Classic Snowman Cookies

Ingredients:

- one cupful (two bars) unsalted butter, softened
- one cupful granulated sugar
- one large egg
- one teaspoonful vanilla extract
- two half cupful all-purpose flour
- half teaspoonful salt
- White fondant (for rolling)
- Royal icing for decorating
- Mini chocolate chips (eyes)
- Orange candy-coated sunflower seeds (carrots)

- Mini pretzels (arms)

Instructions:

1. Butter and sugar should be creamed together in a large basin.
2. Add the egg and vanilla and mix well.
3. Flour and salt should be mixed separately. Mix this up with the butter slowly.
4. Make snowmen with the dough you rolled out.
5. You should bake the cookies on parchment paper.
6. Cook for 8–10 minutes.
7. Once the cookies have cooled, you may decorate them with royal icing and edibles such as micro chocolate chips for the eyes, orange candy-coated sunflower seeds for the carrots, and mini pretzels for the limbs.

Duration: eight-ten minutes

Nutrients (per serving, makes about thirty-six cookies):

- Caloric content: one-fifty
- Fatty acid: six grams
- Carb content: twenty-two grams
- Amino content: one gram

69. Blub Cookies

Ingredients:

- one cupful (two bars) unsalted butter, softened
- one cupful granulated sugar

- one large egg
- one teaspoonful vanilla extract
- two half cupful all-purpose flour
- half teaspoonful salt
- Colored sugars (red, green, yellow, blue)
- Royal icing for decorating

Instructions:

1. Butter and sugar should be creamed together in a large basin.
2. Add the egg and vanilla and mix well.
3. Flour and salt should be mixed separately. Mix this up with the butter slowly.
4. Cut the dough into light bulb shapes by rolling it out.
5. You should bake the cookies on parchment paper.
6. Make each cookie seem like it's lit up with Christmas lights by decorating with different coloured sugars.
7. Cook for 8–10 minutes.
8. After the cookies have cooled, you may add intricate designs with royal icing.

Duration: eight-ten minutes

Nutrients (per serving, makes about thirty-six cookies):

- Caloric content: one-thirty
- Fatty acid: six grams
- Carb content: eighteen grams

- Amino content: one gram

70. Royal Cookies

Ingredients:

- one cupful (two bars) unsalted butter, softened
- one cupful granulated sugar
- one large egg
- one teaspoonful vanilla extract
- two half cupful all-purpose flour
- half teaspoonful salt
- Royal icing for decorating
- Assorted colored sugars and edible decorations

Instructions:

1. Butter and sugar should be creamed together in a large basin.
2. Add the egg and vanilla and mix well.
3. Flour and salt should be mixed separately. Mix this up with the butter slowly.
4. Use a rolling pin to form the dough into nutcrackers.
5. You should bake the cookies on parchment paper.
6. Cook for 8–10 minutes.

7. After the cookies have cooled, you may decorate them in nutcracker patterns using royal icing, colored sugars, and other edible embellishments.

Duration: eight-ten minutes

Nutrients (per serving, makes about thirty-six cookies):

- Caloric content: one-thirty

- Fatty acid: six grams

- Carb content: eighteen grams

- Amino content: one gram

CONCLUSION

As we reach the end of our delightful journey through the "Cookie Cookbook for Beginners," I hope your newfound knowledge and passion for baking cookies will continue to flourish. In this book, we've taken you from being a cookie novice to a confident cookie creator. You've learned the importance of the Joy of Baking and embarked on A Baker's Journey, discovering the wonders of this sweet culinary art form. Armed with the knowledge of Essential Baking Tools and Key Baking Ingredients, you've equipped yourself to create delectable treats. You've mastered the art of Measuring Like a Pro, learned the secrets of Mixing, Stirring, and Folding, and even dived into The Science of Baking, giving you a firm foundation to build upon.

In the chapters on Cookie Fundamentals, we explored the world of Classic Cookie Types, unveiling the secrets of Chocolate Chip Cookies, Sugar Cookies, Oatmeal Raisin Cookies, Peanut Butter Cookies, and Snickerdoodles. The chapter on Cookie

Troubleshooting helped you navigate through common baking pitfalls and showed you how to overcome Texture Issues while Perfecting Flavor.

But this is not the end; rather, it's the beginning of your cookie-baking adventures. The recipes you've collected in the Classic Cookie Creations section are your passport to a world of flavors and textures. Each bite is an opportunity to experience the magic of baking in your own kitchen. Whether you choose to indulge in the time-tested classics or opt for healthy and gluten-free options, you're in for a treat.

As you embark on your baking adventures, remember that cookies are more than just a sweet indulgence. They are a means to connect with loved ones, create cherished memories, and express your creativity. Baking is an art, a science, and a heartfelt gift all in one.

So go ahead, don your apron, Heat in advance the oven, and let the aroma of freshly baked cookies fill your home. Share your creations with friends and family, and relish in the joy that comes from the simple act of sharing something made with love.

Thank you for joining us on this journey through the "Cookie Cookbook for Beginners." May your cookie creations bring happiness and warmth to your life, just as they have to countless others for generations. Happy baking, and may your cookie jar always be full!

Printed in Great Britain
by Amazon